T0163823

BEYOND THE GOLDEN DOOR

ENDORSEMENTS

"*Beyond the Golden Door* by Ali Master is a fascinating study of the American dream, God's great redemption, and the beauty of freedom. In it you will experience the immigrant's journey, a love story inaugurated by fast food, and the ache of longing for a parent's approval. This is an encouraging and interesting read."

—**MARY DeMUTH**, author of *Thin Places: a Memoir*

"I have several reasons for reading Ali Master's autobiographical work, *Beyond the Golden Door*. First, he is a good friend. More importantly, he is a man whose godly character has been demonstrated over a good many years—character I wish to emulate. Beyond this, I really want to know what it is like to walk in the shoes of a foreign student who comes to our shores to receive his education, and who then chooses to embrace the American way of life, with its precious liberties. And, as an American citizen, I am eager to remind myself of the benefits and blessings I possess as a citizen of this great country. Finally, I am interested to learn why a Muslim college student would make the costly decision to become a Christian. I am hopeful that these reasons may also motivate you to read this book."

—**BOB DEFFINBAUGH**, ministry coordinator, Bible.org

"The timing could not have been better for this message to get out. Ali Master's *Beyond the Golden Door* is a refreshing splash of honesty, humor, and gratitude for the American way of life. You and I have likely never viewed the USA through the lens inside these pages."

—**SCOTT LANE**, former chairman of the board, Bill Glass Behind the Walls

"*Beyond the Golden Door* is well written and captivating and provides a frank and revealing look at Ali Master's personal experiences and challenges. This world could use a better understanding of the individuality of life experiences. The assumption that religion follows birthplace and ethnicity is an unconscious bias that many of us fall prey to. This is well worth reading!"

—**KATHERINE HAMMACK**, former United States Assistant Secretary of the Army

"Ali Master shares with us the very personal, inner journey of leaving one world and making his way to a heart-felt, albeit hard-wrung, commitment to his new world. His is an example of how engaging with diversity can transform us if we accept the implicit invitation to transcend the limitations of our own cultural conditioning. Ali welcomed this invitation and embraced the unsettling journey it brought on—challenging and shedding the certainties, conventions, and orthodoxies of his old world. It led him to make courageous and deliberate choices about aspects of life most of us never have to make. Most importantly, it is his sharing with us and taking ownership of the freedoms to fail, love, seek, believe, build, and self-govern that he creates *his* golden door. Ali invites us to celebrate with him, and to cherish and safeguard the essential qualities and conditions that enable everyone to thrive."

—**JÖRG SCHMITZ**, business anthropologist and managing partner, ThomasLeland, author of the *Cultural Orientations Guide*, co-author of *Doing Business Internationally*, and *Leading in English*

"Read this book if you want to be inspired (or re-inspired) about the promise of America. Sometimes we need a reminder from an unexpected source to direct our attention to the treasures that lie right under our noses. *Beyond the Golden Door* does exactly that."

—**DAVID ALEXANDER**, former vice chair, Big 4 Firm

"Into America's debate on immigration and religious liberty, Ali Master's journey is more than one man's story, but a tutorial for all of us on what it means to be truly free. Be ready to be inspired."

—**DR. CRAIG SCHILL**, senior pastor, Lake Cities Community Church and adjunct professor, Dallas Theological Seminary

"We celebrate the freedoms guaranteed by the Constitution, but few appreciate the freedoms that are the fabric of our culture. Ali Master reveals them through his journey to embrace them, reflecting upon the events and influences that guided his discovery. He engages us with good storytelling, humor, generous thanks for God's gracious providence—and offers us tested wisdom to better understand ourselves and our world."

—**DR. TIM RALSTON**, professor of pastoral ministries, Dallas Theological Seminary

"Whether you are curious about God, intrigued by the draw of the American dream, inspired by those who have overcome great challenges or just enjoy a compelling read, I heartily recommend *Beyond the Golden Door* by Ali Master. Having only known Ali as the successful businessman and deeply committed follower of Christ that he is today, I have been inspired beyond description by the journey that led him to not only discover, but also embrace the American freedoms so easily taken for granted. Through these words, I have found myself challenged to live with a deeper appreciation for my faith and my freedoms."

—**ANN E. BRADSHAW**, partner, Big 4 Firm

Seeing the American Dream Through an Immigrant's Eyes

BEYOND THE GOLDEN DOOR

ALI MASTER

NEW YORK

LONDON • NASHVILLE • MELBOURNE • VANCOUVER

BEYOND THE GOLDEN DOOR

Seeing the American Dream through an Immigrant's Eyes

© 2019 Ali Master

All rights reserved. No portion of this book may be reproduced, stored in a retrieval system, or transmitted in any form or by any means—electronic, mechanical, photocopy, recording, scanning, or other—except for brief quotations in critical reviews or articles, without the prior written permission of the publisher.

Published in New York, New York, by Morgan James Publishing. Morgan James is a trademark of Morgan James, LLC. www.MorganJamesPublishing.com

ISBN 9781642792850 paperback
ISBN 9781642792567 case laminate hard cover
ISBN 9781642792874 eBook
Library of Congress Control Number: 2018911340

Cover & Interior Design by:
Christopher Kirk
www.GFSstudio.com

Unless otherwise noted, all scripture citations are from the New International Version (NIV) Holy Bible, New International Version®, NIV® Copyright ©1973, 1978, 1984, 2011 by Biblica, Inc.® Used by permission. All rights reserved worldwide.

Other Bible translations cited include:
Contemporary English Version (CEV). Copyright © 1995 by American Bible Society.
Good News Translation (GNT). Copyright © 1992 by American Bible Society
International Standard Version (ISV). Copyright © 1995-2014 by ISV Foundation. ALL RIGHTS RESERVED INTERNATIONALLY. Used by permission of Davidson Press, LLC.
New King James Version (NKJV). Scripture taken from the New King James Version®. Copyright © 1982 by Thomas Nelson. Used by permission. All rights reserved.
The Message (MSG). Copyright © 1993, 1994, 1995, 1996, 2000, 2001, 2002 by Eugene H. Peterson.

Song Lyrics:
THE HEART OF ROCK AND ROLL
Words and Music by JOHNNY COLLA and HUEY LEWIS
Copyright © 1983 WB MUSIC CORP., HUEY LEWIS MUSIC and CAUSE & EFFECT MUSIC
All Rights Administered by WB MUSIC CORP.
All Rights Reserved
Used By Permission of ALFRED MUSIC

Morgan James is a proud partner of Habitat for Humanity Peninsula and Greater Williamsburg. Partners in building since 2006.

Get involved today! Visit
MorganJamesPublishing.com/giving-back

DISCLAIMER

The events portrayed in this memoir are represented to the best of my recollection. While the stories in this book are true, some names and identifying details have been modified to preserve anonymity. Likewise, the conversations are not written to represent word-for-word transcripts. Instead, I have retold them in a way that induces the sentiment and significance of what was said; however, the substance of the dialogue is accurate.

DEDICATION

To my wife, Judy, who forever changed the trajectory of my life.
And to my children: Mollie, Noah, Emma and Isaac—may you
each find and live your own American Dream.

TABLE OF CONTENTS

ACKNOWLEDGEMENTS

There are several individuals whom I must thank, without whose efforts you would not be holding this book in its current state.

I am eternally grateful to my wife Judy who painstakingly reviewed my initial drafts and made many important suggestions. It always amazed me how much smarter she made me sound. Thank you for believing in me. The biggest compliment I can give you is that, 27 years later, I still want to impress you.

Many thanks to my editor James Pence, who helped me believe I could write this book on my own without the aid of a ghostwriter. James also helped market my book proposal, which was ultimately accepted by Morgan James.

A special thanks to Craig and Tammy Schill for taking my manuscript with them on their Africa trip and giving me their invaluable feedback.

My son Noah used his talents to design my author website. Thanks, Son!

Thanks also go to Noah Totten of Ark Motion Media for his contributions to this project. You two make an amazing team.

My love language is words of affirmation.[1] I have received encouragement from many people throughout this book-writing process. Their words have served as indispensable fuel for me, enabling me to carry on while juggling numerous other responsibilities. A heartfelt thanks to the following friends, family, and colleagues who took the time to read early copies of the book and share their positive feedback:

My in-laws, John and Jean Fox, for your steadfast support as I wrote the book.

My sister-in-law, Suzy Fox, for reading the book while caring for three young boys.

My dear EY colleagues Ann Bradshaw, Julie Gallina, Leigh Messina, Kristie Lowery, Tim Parrish, Brad Withrow, Debra von Storch, Gopika Parikh, Katherine Hammack, Bridgette Long, Stephen Kenney, Kathy Collins, and Lori Maite. It means the world to me that you created space in your busy careers and lives to read my book and provide amazing validation.

Stephanie Del Paggio for sharing her millennial point of view.

Thank you to each member of the Morgan James staff that worked on the project. I could not have asked for a more affirming group of consummate professionals.

Dr. Tim Ralston for his support and thought provoking feedback about the key takeaways of the book.

Thank you also to the following Ernst & Young quality and risk management professionals for their guidance: Ted Acosta, Sue Meyer, Michele Geist, and Joe Sullivan.

Finally, to all those who have taught me something along the way about faith, leadership, inclusion, and persistence. You know who you are. Thank you.

ℐNTRODUCTION

On August 25th, 2018, America witnessed the passing of one of its celebrated war heroes and statesmen in Senator John McCain. I didn't always agree with his political views; however, as I read the tributes from both allies and adversaries, what jumped out most to me was his unreserved confidence in American exceptionalism.

One quote, in which Senator McCain discussed his own captivity by the North Vietnamese, struck a special cord with me:

> In prison, I fell in love with my country. I had loved her before then, but like most young people, my affection was little more than a simple appreciation for the comforts and privileges most Americans enjoyed and took for granted. It wasn't until I had lost America for a time that I realized how much I loved her.[2]

In many ways, this book echoes the same message: to remind Americans about the liberties we all enjoy and often take for granted. The lens John McCain was forced to use to gain his powerful insight was captivity. The lens I use is my own personal immigrant journey of experiencing freedom—both its absence in the nations I grew up in and its abundance in America.

At its core, *Beyond the Golden Door* is about two primary themes. First, I want to take you, the reader, along on a journey of a young immigrant who experiences the American Dream with all its promise, freedoms, and challenges. I also want to extol the virtues of specific freedoms we all cherish in the USA, comparing and contrasting them to life lived in other countries, and tracing them back to their source: our values. Second is the theme of a sovereign Creator that works in the lives of men and nations. It's my objective that as you read about my American experience, it will lead you to some thoughtful introspection and examination of your own life journey. I believe that there are no accidents.

Why Now?

We are facing a range of complex threats and challenges today including nationalism leading to potential racism, the dilemma of immigration, terrorism, and an increasingly polarized nation divided around the efficacy of capitalism. Many are asking essential questions such as: Is the American Dream still alive? To whom does America belong? Are the values upon which this nation was founded still relevant? Can immigrants, especially those from Muslim nations, effectively assimilate into American culture? And is American democracy portable?

I wrote this book because I feel strongly that everyday Americans could benefit from a Muslim-background immigrant's perspective on these questions. While this may sound a tad academic, you will be relieved to hear that it's not. This is a story that contains all the themes of human life: love, family, faith, failure, and redemption.

There are four parts to my book:

Part I recounts my life growing up in Pakistan in a devout Shia Muslim home, including the culture, customs, and politics. You'll learn about my family and some dark secrets from my life that I am bringing to light because they are relevant to how I am wired. Certain traumatic events in my formative years shaped my future in unexpected ways, and I will share those with you.

Part II contains true stories about the many misconceptions and stereotypes we immigrants bring with us about how life in America is supposed to work. These will make you laugh (mostly) and shake your head in disbelief. You will discover that culture shock is real, and in my case, downright dangerous at times.

Part III focuses on five precious American freedoms I experienced: **failure, love, religion, entrepreneurship,** and **government.** Some of these came at great personal risk and you will feel both the joy and pain of what I went through as I lived out each of these liberties.

Part IV asks some important questions that we should all consider: Where do these amazing freedoms come from? What kind of person thrives in this free environment? And most importantly, what should be our response to them?

Why Me?

So, why should you listen to *me*? As I have already mentioned, this is not meant to be an academic book that tries to solve our nation's problems. People a lot smarter than I am aspire to do that and, frankly, they're not getting very far. No, this book is a humble reminder from an uninvited alien to ordinary Americans about the greatness—albeit somewhat diminished—we still possess. That said, I have personally experienced the unique combination of the five American freedoms I highlight in this book. After having lived over thirty-two years in America and another nineteen in three other nations, having experienced two world religions, and having founded and owned multiple small and large successful businesses, I believe I can give you an honest and first-hand assessment of the American Dream.

What Are the Takeaways?

> *The mission of this book is to communicate that being an American is not about ethnicity, religion, or the color of your skin. Rather, it's a state of mind. It is our shared values and freedoms that make us uniquely American.*

As you read this book, it is my hope that you will:
- Gain (or regain) an appreciation of five transformational freedoms we enjoy in America: freedom of failure (to start-over), religion, love (discovering your mate), to build (entrepreneurship), and to self-govern (government). Understand the uniqueness of American values as they are contrasted to those found elsewhere, namely, the East.
- Understand where these precious freedoms and values come from, why they are hard to replicate, and why they are worth preserving, fighting and dying for.

- Ultimately, you will also discover that this tale is about God, the true source of liberty, and how He works in people's lives to bring about unexpected and undeserved redemption.

How Did This Book Come About?

Beyond the Golden Door has been a work in progress over the past eighteen years. In the 1990s, I was one of the first Muslim Background Believers (MBBs) in my state. This was well before 9/11, and America was not as sensitized to Islam as perhaps it is today. During those years, I had at least one serious offer to pen my story alongside a well-known Christian personality. However, deep down inside, I wanted to share the stories myself. In addition, the entrepreneur in me longed to see if I could make it on my own.

As time passed, the idea of a book on the American Dream was further cemented in my mind. Plenty of MBBs had written their conversion stories, and there was absolutely nothing wrong with that. I wanted my book to be about something on a grander scale. I wanted to explore the environment of freedom that enabled me and many of my fellow MBBs to consider alternative truth without fear of persecution—or worse.

I made two significant discoveries as I worked on this project. First, I realized how much America has changed over the past three decades. We are more polarized as a nation, and have drifted further away from America's fundamental values, the bedrock of our founding. Second, I gained an acute awareness of how extremely blessed I have been. This was quite easy to see once I reviewed the sequence of events of my life as I wrote this book. Yet even as I became aware of the blessings I have received, I am also conscious of the challenges I face.

For a long time now, I have had to walk a fine line, whether at work, with my extended Muslim family, or in social circles of former classmates. The fine line I speak of is being authentic with who I am, yet not offending others. Muslim societies are collective in nature. Unanimity takes precedence over individualism. This is especially problematic when your worldview is diametrically opposed to the society at large. I have long struggled with how my colleagues at work will view the exercise of my individual freedom, or how sharing my story might offend or hurt my Muslim relatives and friends. I want them to know that I love them deeply and want them to experience the same peace and joy I have by learning about the real identity of Jesus Christ and His love for them.

In the final analysis, I feel telling the truth about my views and beliefs is more important than polite silence. If my story can change the point-of-view of even one person, then it has been worth the risk.

Conclusion

The fabric of American culture is changing rapidly, often being shaped by fear. Fear is a powerful force. It drives us toward our natural inclination: self-preservation. I am concerned that the political turmoil we are witnessing could lead America to a circle-the-wagons mentality and even to the curtailments of certain rights for select people-groups. I believe that such actions could be like releasing the proverbial genie from the bottle and would be impossible to recapture.

On the other hand, the terror events, the constant hate rhetoric we hear against America, the past defections to ISIS by Westerners, and the apologies and appeasements made to other nations by some of our political leaders might cause some to wonder whether those who hate us are right. Maybe America isn't such a special nation after all. Maybe others do have the right to hate us.

In this book I share why I believe those thoughts are incorrect. I want Americans to understand that not everyone who comes from a Muslim country hates the USA. Hopefully my story and the freedoms I outline will motivate you to share the same American values and truths with other immigrants coming into the United States that I discovered many years ago.

My hope is that you will be proud to be an American and value those same freedoms. And if you are not an American already, perhaps this book will make you want to become one.

Enjoy the read. Come see the American Dream through an immigrant's eyes.

"Give me your tired, your poor,
Your huddled masses yearning to breathe free,
The wretched refuse of your teeming shore,
Send these, the homeless, tempest-tost, to me,
I lift my lamp beside the golden door!"[3]

Emma Lazarus

PART I

The Journey
There

Chapter 1

ALWIDA (GOODBYE),
MY CITY OF LIGHTS

May 12th, 1986

It was going to be the longest day of my eighteen-year life.

After being surrounded by people all day long, I was finally alone. Well, almost. I was surrounded by about 300 passengers in the huge, Scandinavian Airlines (SAS) 747 I had boarded at Karachi's Jinnah International Airport. Of those 300 people, I knew only one.

Much to my chagrin, Mr. Fahim Khan, my friend Ahmed's father, had chosen to accompany me on the same flight. Not that I minded having an elder accompanying me on what would be the farthest I had ever travelled internationally, but I had to be careful when speaking about Ahmed so as not to blow his secret.

Ahmed was gay. And his parents, like most Pakistani parents, had no idea. Having Mr. Khan with me all the way to New York, not to mention an eight-hour layover in Copenhagen, was going to make for an interesting day. Fortunately, our seats were not close to each other.

It had been a long day already and we hadn't even begun our thirty-hour journey from Karachi to Dubai, then Copenhagen to New York, and finally to Dallas, Texas. I couldn't believe the day was finally here. I was leaving for America.

I had been working toward this goal for almost two years, and it had been an arduous process. First, I'd tried to enroll in a university in Karachi, but with only two engineering schools in a city of sixteen million coupled with my mediocre grades—apparently, they didn't offer extra credit for table-tennis and cricket— that didn't happen. My focus shifted to studying in America, but the first and largest hurdle was convincing my mother, whom I called Ammi.

3

I was an only child, and this would not be an easy sell. "It's only four years, Ammi. I will come back," I promised.

In the 1950s, Ammi had herself gone to London as a single Muslim woman. In fact, she was one of the first women to ever attend a university in Karachi. She was a genuine trailblazer. Finally, with my father's insistence, she begrudgingly granted my request.

My father, whom I called Abboo, was a gentle and quiet man. He had worked for the same company, an affiliate of General Electric, for over thirty-five years. In lieu of his pension, Abboo requested that the company

Me (around age 20)

My parents: Abboo and Ammi

sponsor my education in the United States. He traded his entire pension for a letter of support and one year's worth of tuition payable to the University of Texas at Arlington.

Having some US Embassy contacts didn't hurt, either. The two boys interviewing ahead of me both left with tears in their eyes, their dreams shattered.

"This is a good school," the tall, blonde American interviewer had said as she stamped my passport. With this single act of approval, my life had been changed. I was heading to America. I will never forget the look on Abboo's face when I emerged from the Karachi US Embassy after my visa interview. I jiggled my head sideways, confirming that I had indeed been awarded the prized stamp. His expression reflected simultaneous relief and pain.

Abboo succeeded in achieving a critical goal that all Pakistani parents—really, parents everywhere—have for their children: to give them a chance for a better education and future than *they* had. But my father's joy was mixed with sadness. He had already begun processing the grief of my leaving.

His look saddened me, but the excitement of traveling to Texas quickly swept these feelings away. All at once, I had literally hundreds of details to plan with very little knowledge of America to guide me aside from *Archie Comics*.

This was 1986, and long before the internet. I was flying blind and using whatever resources I could find. But somehow I finished all the planning and was now on my way.

As the 747 began taxiing, I settled in for the long flight to Copenhagen via Dubai. It was midnight—most international flights depart Karachi at ungodly hours—but I was too excited to be sleepy. As the jumbo jet ascended on this cloudless night, I took in the breathtaking view of the millions of lights of Karachi.

Her citizens often refer to Karachi as the City of Lights. At midnight on a Saturday, things are just getting warmed up. Barbecue restaurants bustle with customers sitting outside on street tables with waiters weaving in and out among them bearing delicious *chicken tikkas* and *sheesh kabobs*. Fresh *tandoori naans* (traditional bread made in clay ovens) are being served along with the traditional *chai* (tea). Cricket matches are being played under the lights. Ladies are bargaining with shopkeepers for ornately embroidered clothes, bangles, shoes and more. Rickshaws, buses, donkey carts, and the occasional Mercedes all make their way amid the crawling traffic.

Karachi at night

I smiled a melancholy smile and bid farewell to Karachi, my City of Lights.

The very foreign-sounding flight attendant came on the PA to welcome us on board and provide details of our journey to Copenhagen. The first announcements were in Danish, which few understood, since most were Urdu-speaking Pakistanis. About twenty percent of the crowd, those belonging to the upper crust of Karachi society, comprehended the English announcement. Finally, another flight attendant spoke in Urdu, the national language. Ironically, the Pakistanis who understood the English announcement would barely comprehend this Urdu version. Pakistan is a land of haves and have-nots, with no middle class to speak of. The elite control everything, and the gap has only widened in recent years.

Since the captain had now switched off the seat belt sign, I tried to get comfortable in my coach window seat. I looked out the window hoping to catch a last glimpse of the fading lights of my home city.

It was here in Karachi that I was born in 1967. I was an only child, but I didn't learn the true details of my birth until I was sixteen. I had been told that Ammi and Abboo had married late. She had graduated with a degree in botany and taught for eight years in the Karachi Women's College while he shouldered the burden of supporting his seven sisters, two brothers, and my widowed grandmother (or *Dadi-Ma* as we all called her). By the time a marriage arrangement was settled, Ammi was in her thirties and Abboo in his early forties, making them both ancient by Pakistani standards when it came to the idea of marriage.

After my birth, my parents moved immediately to Dhaka, Bangladesh, which was then part of East Pakistan. If there was one thing Abboo was passionate about, it was business. Dhaka was booming and needed Western Pakistanis to come invest. The local Bengalis provided ample cheap labor.

We lived in a large, two-story bungalow with a huge front lawn. The land-lord resided on the first floor and we stayed on the ground floor. The bungalow included some facilities in the rear that served as servant quarters. These quarters accommodated our cook Joseph, several maids, and the chauffeur.

Things were going well until 1971, when war broke out with India[4], the arch-rival of Pakistan. At the same time, East Pakistan seceded to become an inde-pendent state. The local Bengalis, long-suppressed by West Pakistanis, were ready to avenge themselves. Several Bengalis invaded our neighborhood, ready to burn alive any non-Bengali-speaking people.

I was four years old. My mother had to tightly cover my mouth with her *dupatta* (the traditional head covering worn by women) to ensure I did

With Abboo in Dhaka at age 6 months

A happy toddler

not cry out. Thank God for our Bengali landlord who sent the mob away, telling them that no one was left in the house but Bengalis. We left everything in Dhaka, catching one of the last possible flights west to Karachi and from there to the ancient city of Lahore.

Laid out by the Mughal Dynasty emperors in the mid-to-late 1600s, Lahore is Pakistan's most historic city, famous for its castles, major mosques, and gardens. Aurangzeb, the son of King Shah Jahan, who had the Taj-Mahal built in the memory of his beautiful wife, Mumtaz, oversaw much of the construction in Lahore.[5]

Historic City of Lahore

The city had an air of leisure, its pace far slower and more relaxed than what I would experience in Karachi seven years later. If Karachi was like the New York City of Southeast Asia, then Lahore was like Richmond or Indianapolis.

We spent seven years in Lahore and most of my childhood memories were made there. My father was the managing director of his company's branch and we maintained a very comfortable lifestyle. The company paid for our housing, car, and even a membership at the *gymkhana* (country club).

Fashionable at 4

First bike

With Ammi in Lahore at age 6

We lived in a nice bungalow in the Gulberg area, an established part of Lahore. Our neighbors included a German family on one side and the founder of RC Cola on the other. It was a quiet place with big metal gates, tall walls, and security guards posted outside the larger homes.

I attended Cathedral High School, a private coeducational school. The name might sound a bit unusual for the Islamic Republic of Pakistan, but many of the educational institutions had their roots in pre-partition British colonial India. Both Pakistan and India received their independence in 1947 from Great Britain.[6]

Once a week, I would enjoy horseback riding and then we would go to the *gymkhana* on the weekends for swimming and snacks. I even had my own dog, a mixed-breed named Ponti that spent his nights inside our home, a rare privilege for dogs in Muslim countries since they are considered unclean.[7]

I smiled at the memory of my first and only dog, but my smile faded as I recalled how he died.

I found him lying in the backyard, foaming at the mouth. It was the middle of the day and Abboo had not yet returned from the office. I ran to Ammi screaming for help, but she could do nothing. Her religion did not allow her to touch the dog. I picked him up and rushed outside to hail a rickshaw to deliver Ponti to the vet. I tearfully urged the rickshaw driver to hurry while Ponti's movements slowed down and eventually stopped completely. I was only ten years old and had no business being in a rickshaw driven by a stranger several miles from home with a dead dog in my arms.

The peace and tranquility of Lahore had been an illusion. As I think back to my seven years there, much had happened, or perhaps more importantly, did not happen, that haunts me to this day.

My recollections were interrupted by the captain's announcement that we would be landing in Dubai soon. We landed smoothly, and the mostly-Pakistani laborers disembarked into Dubai replaced by a completely different-looking group of Scandinavian, Arab, and US-bound American passengers. With the new passengers on board, we took off for Copenhagen.

I settled in for the six-hour jaunt to Denmark, the longest flight of my life. I was thankful that the elderly Pakistani man in the seat next to me was already dozing off. I should try to do the same, I thought. But my mind raced back to Lahore.

I had a lot of time on my hands as a young boy. As an only child, I was often forced to entertain myself and developed a keen interest in the game of cricket, testing my skills against several neighbor boys and our cook, John. I remember Abboo asking me if I wanted to go watch a live match at the famous Gaddafi Stadium, named in honor of Libyan dictator, Muammar Gaddafi, only a few miles from our home. We went to the stadium and watched forty-thousand rabid fans root for the home team. I can't recall exactly who we were playing, but I can only surmise it was India due to the intense reactions from the fans.

India was our enemy. The fact that the border between the two countries was only sixty-six kilometers (about forty-one miles) away in Amritsar was not lost on me. I noticed many fans wearing Sikh turbans and many Hindus waving Indian flags in the stands—a highly ill-advised move, even from an eleven-year-old's perspective.

The stadium lived up to its namesake's reputation and by two o'clock, there was a rift between the two fan groups. The police tried unsuccessfully to protect the visiting team's fans, and soon I had my first and only exposure to tear gas. I remember Abboo grabbing my hand and doing his best to get us both out of the stadium in one piece. My eyes burned, and I was confused. I couldn't understand how things had escalated to this point. Nor can I recall if the match was ever completed.

The tensions between the two countries remained high, and in May of 1974, India proudly detonated its first nuclear device, initiating the arms race between the two nations. Due to Amritsar being so close, it wasn't unusual for us to hear sirens when unofficial skirmishes took place on the border.

I would learn during my remaining life in Pakistan, safety is a relative term.

One Sunday afternoon, following a leisurely lunch and swim at the local Lahore *gymkhana*, we were all headed home in our 1964 Chevy II—we had one of the only American cars in the city—when there was yet another reminder of the precarious times in which we lived. As we pulled into our driveway, we saw a low-flying Pakistan Air Force (PAF) jet chasing what appeared to be an Indian fighter jet. A split second later, we heard a thunderous explosion, and a soldier standing on our front lawn yelled at us to stay in our vehicle and get down.

Although the event was over in a matter of seconds, it pierced the thin veneer of security I thought I lived in. I began to wonder just how safe this world was. Sadly, I would learn during my remaining life in Pakistan, safety is a relative term.

I looked at my watch to check how long we had been flying. Between my napping, reminiscing, and eating multiple times, four hours had passed since we left Karachi. I decided that the food was one of the things I liked best about international travel thus far.

Four more hours to Copenhagen, I thought excitedly.

Seeing Europe was a big event in my book, even though I would never leave the airport. As far as I was concerned, it still counted. I shot a quick glance at Mr. Khan six rows ahead to see if he was awake. He was still asleep, his sleeping mask covering his eyes. With two of his boys already in Jersey City, he was a veteran international traveler. That was good, since it gave me more time to plot my strategy for dodging questions that might come my way about Ahmed. I grimaced at the similarities I saw between Mr. Khan and my own parents. I wondered if he knew as little about his own son as Ammi and Abboo knew about me.

My thoughts went back to Cathedral High School. It was not at all uncommon for Muslim students from upper-class families to attend schools established by the Catholic Church and run by nuns. We were a former British Colony, after all. Nevertheless, during the religion period on a school day, the Muslim students would go to an Islam class while the very few others, whether they were Christian, Hindu, or Zoroastrian (Parsi, as they were called), would learn civics.

The Muslim parents were not concerned in the least that their children would be exposed to non-Islamic theology. We were all taught from a very young age that although Allah sent one hundred and twenty-four thousand prophets since the start of this world—and Isa (Jesus) was certainly one of them—Mohammed brought the perfect and final revelation of Allah in Islam. There was never a reason to question this fact. Besides, all our house help: the cook, the chauffeur, and the maids considered themselves Christian. Minorities were almost exclusively on the bottom rung of the social and economic ladder, further evidence of the superiority of Islam.

I remember only a few things about my school experience in Lahore. First was the joy it brought Abboo when I ranked second in my third-grade class. He glowed for days after seeing my report card. That was when I understood how important education was to him.

A less-pleasant memory was a strict rule that prohibited students from going to the bathroom during class. There were no exceptions. If you had too much to drink in the morning, you were doomed. Many a kid would squirm for hours in his or her seat before racing for the door in desperation. When the student returned, the teacher would cane the student in front of everyone for disrupting the class. Caning was not the only form of punishment. It was not at all unusual for a teacher to slap a student. This miserable experience reminded me that I was unsafe outside my home.

I remember sneaking into the cathedral portion of the school around Christmas and admiring the beautiful stained-glass windows. The artwork on the walls depicting Mary and the Christ child fascinated me. In Islam, it was forbidden to paint pictures of any revered characters. I heard a group of people clad in robes singing *Gloria in Excelsis Deo*. I had no idea what they were singing, but I felt warm and liked the sound of it very much. That comforting feeling from being in the church stayed with me for many years.

I would go horseback riding at least once a week. The *ghora-wala* (horseman) whose name was Jamil would bring a horse named Brownie every Tuesday afternoon after school and we would go for a ride in a nearby field. One day, Brownie was feeling frisky. Jamil was distracted and didn't pay attention to the very large, ornate truck that pulled up beside Brownie and me at a traffic light.

In Pakistan, trucks are the *rajas* (princes) of the road. Brightly-colored, with pictures, poetry, and chimes to make them look and sound interesting, they are known for their very loud horns. Unlike most Western societies where one honks the horn to alert others of danger, Pakistani drivers blare their horns for the sheer thrill of it.

It was the loudest and longest horn blast I'd ever heard.

Brownie reared up and took off like a racehorse, with me clinging to him for dear life. I eventually fell off but wasn't seriously hurt. Jamil never came again after dropping me home. I simply went to my room, hid my torn and dirty shirt, and went about my business. I never rode Brownie again after that day.

I looked at my watch. Only an hour and thirty minutes to Copenhagen. The flight monitor on the big screen on the center aisle wall showed how far we had flown. My heart raced as the plane began its descent. The old man next to me was still enjoying his slumber. I was thankful. I had too much going through my mind to chit-chat with anyone, especially an elder.

My thoughts raced back to the final chapters in Lahore—the ones I did not want to think about. If the stability on the outside was a façade, then inside the tall walls of my bungalow in Lahore was a trap of another variety. First, there was Francis, a seventeen-year-old hired by my parents to assist the chef and help with various household chores. One afternoon, Francis suddenly closed the door to my playroom. He started to undress himself and asked me to pretend to be his "doctor." As an innocent eleven-year-old, I found this quite humorous and let out a loud chuckle.

Ammi was a light sleeper. She either heard or suspected something because before things could go any further, she barged into the playroom. "What is going on here?" she demanded. She then grabbed a broomstick and proceeded to beat me. Fortunately, Ammi lacked eye-hand coordination and I wasn't hurt severely, but the emotional damage inflicted was another story.

I was perplexed and confused for days. Did I do something wrong? Ammi's fury suggested as much. Did I encourage this bad behavior from Francis? Surely I must have.

Francis was fired, and I never saw him again. For days afterwards, Ammi would lecture me about the evils of sex. I had no idea what sex was, but I decided that whatever it was, it was something Allah hated.

About six months after the episode with Francis, there was another incident with John, one of the cooks that moved from Dhaka to Lahore with us. John was about twenty. Not having any siblings or organized sports to keep me busy, and with minimal supervision from my mother during the day, I sometimes visited the servant quarters at the back of our property. One day, John and I were playing a game. It might have been Snakes and Ladders or *Ludo* (our version of Sorry!). The room was a tad dark and reeked with the musky scent of the unwashed quilt on John's *char-pai* (a cot made of rope). When he touched me, it was like an electric shock went through me. I raced home from John's quarters crying. Something in my eleven-year-old mind knew instinctively that what he tried to do was very wrong. But I didn't tell Ammi this time. There was no chance that I was going to risk being beaten again. Going to my father did not even occur to me. He was so quiet and passive that I couldn't imagine talking about something so personal with him.

> *I truly believed that hiding was for the best, and that dealing with problems alone was normal.*

I determined that such matters had to be faced alone. This was a personal issue between me and my offender. I determined never to be alone with John again. For his part, John never approached me again. But several others did. They were all the same— older boys that were hired by my unassuming parents. By this time, though, I had become wise to the ways of such predators.

It became almost a vicious game. My parents hired someone; he befriended me; then at some point, he would venture into the inappropriate. It might be stories, innuendo, questions, pictures, or more. I developed a keen radar for such men, some of whom reached further in their lustful pursuits with me than others. I couldn't evade them all. I was only eleven after all. These incidents, and my evasive maneuvers, became my personal secrets—ones my naïve and uninvolved parents couldn't have imagined. I truly believed that hiding was for the best, and that dealing with problems alone was normal.

I learned to survive at an early age. Here in the plane, many miles away from John, Francis, and the broomstick, I grimaced as I knew that I was not alone in my experience. The challenges I faced were the norm for many boys in my country.

It was life in Pakistan.

I have the executed Prime Minister, Zulfikar Ali Bhutto[8], to thank for my escape from the cage that was Lahore. In April of 1979, two years after a coup d'état by General Zia ul-Haq, Bhutto was hanged. This execution led to riots which cast such a pall on the already-faltering economy that Abboo's company immediately requested a transfer back to Karachi.

We were returning to my birth city. This is where all my cousins, aunts and uncles lived. I was thrilled. I remember thinking that perhaps Karachi would give me a fresh start. But Karachi, as I would soon learn, would only serve to fast-track my life lessons. At the ripe old age of twelve, life was headed from PG-13 to R.

The captain came on the PA to instruct the flight attendants to prepare the cabin for landing. I focused my attention on the new experience of time-zone changes. It was 3 AM in Copenhagen, but 9 AM in Karachi. We had been travelling westward for over nine hours. Since it was dark, I could only admire the lights of the capital of Denmark.

I was still excited to catch whatever sights I could and braced myself for the landing. The SAS 747 landed as smoothly as it had taken off. A round of applause broke out from a group of Danish students returning home from Dubai. I was ready to stretch my legs. A few rows up, Mr. Khan was showing signs of life. The old man next to me was already telling me which luggage he wanted me to get up and grab for him. We arrived at the gate and made our way into the very clean and shiny Kastrup Airport terminal.

Chapter 2
IN THE THIRD WORLD NO MORE

*A*s we deplaned at Kastrup, I could now appreciate why they call places like Pakistan the Third World. Everything here looked spotless. The floor had been recently waxed. The airport staff were prim and proper, with well-marked, tidy uniforms. There were clear directions in both Danish and English for travelers to follow. A lady in a neat blue SAS uniform directed Mr. Khan and me to the transit lounge where we were to spend the long layover.

I was impressed.

It was the wee hours of the morning in Copenhagen, so the airport was not crowded. We slowly made our way to the transit lounge and sat on the clean, comfortable leather chairs. My heart was racing. I was in Europe. It was a shame we had no time to go see the sights.

We made idle chit-chat, but fortunately Mr. Khan wanted to continue his slumber. That was fine with me. His son Ahmed and I had known each other for about five years. He was well-versed in American culture since two of his brothers and a sister already lived in the States.

I remember flipping through the *GQ* magazines that his brothers sent back. Ahmed loved fashion. His sister would also record the weekly radio program *Top 40* and mail the audio tapes to him. On weekends when I would visit Ahmed's home, I would hear host Casey Kasem announce the biggest pop hits of the week. It was like being transported into another world. And here I was, getting closer by the hour to that world.

Ahmed had begun to act differently over the past few years. His demeanor changed, and I didn't fully understand what was going on with him. As teenage

17

boys, we would both go out to socialize with the other upper-middle-class and wealthy kids. While I was primarily interested in trying to impress the girls, I noticed that Ahmed had no interest in them, even though they got along well, and he did not appear to experience the awkwardness I felt. I was jealous of that.

A few months before my departure, Ahmed told me he was gay. Somehow, I had known. It was a sad situation for Ahmed, because Karachi is not the kind of place where you can be open about such things. His parents had no idea and I planned to keep it that way for his sake.

After a few hours, I decided to check out the ice cream parlor located on the west side of the transit lounge. I gaped at the prices listed in dollars and immediately converted them into rupees in my head. Fifty-five rupees for a single scoop of strawberry ice cream? It would have only cost five rupees in Karachi. I was starving, so I splurged anyway. The ice cream was indeed delicious, but certainly wasn't the equivalent of eleven scoops of Pakistani ice cream.

As I walked around the lounge, I noticed things other than the cleanliness and the prices. People didn't make eye contact as they walked by. Pakistani and Muslim culture in general is a staring culture. You tend to make eye contact and sometimes hold your gaze a little longer than you should. No one looked at me here. I almost felt invisible. I didn't know how I felt about that just yet. I also noticed that men and women showed affection more openly. I saw one college-age couple walking hand-in-hand. The girl wore tight jeans and his hand was around her waist. Another couple was kissing in the restaurant. All of this was foreign to me. I had seen it in American movies, of course, but to be surrounded by it was altogether surreal.

> *In the West, it seemed, even package movers had rights, respect, and dignity.*

Later that afternoon, I got an inkling of why the ice cream was more expensive than back home and I discovered a significant difference between how the West treats their laborers versus the East. I was watching the planes pulling in and out of the gates when I noticed one area on the tarmac where a lot of packages were neatly stacked on a pallet. An Asian man, dressed in orange coveralls, was moving the packages using a mechanical forklift. He wore gloves, goggles, and ear plugs. He drove the forklift, efficiently picking up packages and moving them to a truck. He seemed to be in a rhythm, enjoying the task set before him.

In Pakistan, this back-breaking job would have been done by a handful of laborers with their bare hands, taking ten times as long. They would be paid next-to-nothing for their toil. In the West, it seemed, even package movers had rights, respect, and dignity.

As I walked around the airport, I ventured into a news and magazine shop. I noticed how everything was organized and had a set price on it. In Pakistan, especially in an airport where you have unsuspecting tourists, shopkeepers never put the price on an object for sale. Instead, they throw out a price in the hopes that the buyer may just be foolish enough to pay it. Some do, in which case, they would graciously offer the person a Coca-Cola while they packaged the item.

But most of the time, the shopkeepers were not so fortunate, and people like my mother would brush off their originally stated price with a stunningly-low counter offer. I watched my Ammi in awe and admiration, wondering how she made such an offer with a straight face. Her offer would trigger an instant litany of pleadings from the shopkeeper, referring to everything from his child's education to his sick wife as reasons why they needed to, at least, meet in the middle.

Ammi had ice in her veins when it came to such matters and would start to leave the shop stating, *"Na-hi bhai"* (No, brother). Just before we walked out the door, the shopkeeper would then yell out a price that was usually seventy-five percent of the original offer. Ammi would then complete the transaction and we would move on to torture our next victim. That is how purchasing was done in Pakistan.

However, here in Copenhagen, I found the photos on magazine covers far more shocking than the exorbitant prices. How could their government allow these shop owners to sell such things?

I remembered the promise I had made to Allah. I promised to be a good Muslim and to pray 100 *rakat* (repetitious prayers) to repay Allah for allowing me to get this all-important visa to the States. I decided to leave the tempting magazine covers behind and go see if Mr. Khan had awakened from his nap. We only had a few more hours before heading to New York.

Mr. Khan was awake and had purchased some snacks for us. We talked mostly about nothing. He was very proud of his sons and was excited to visit New Jersey for the third time. Occasionally he would throw out a probing question about which girls in the neighborhood liked Ahmed. I was prepared for such queries and adeptly deflected them by saying, "Oh, Uncle, we only study together and then play cricket with the boys." Mr. Khan wasn't my actual uncle, but in Pakistani culture everyone was respectfully called *uncle* or *aunty* regardless of whether they were related to you.

Finally, it was time to board our flight to New York. I was exhausted from the eight-hour layover with no sleep, but my heart beat even faster as we began the final leg of our journey to America. Fortunately, I was again separated from Mr. Khan, who was upgraded to business class. I trudged to the back of the SAS Airbus and found my seat. The plane was mostly full, but not as crowded as coming from Dubai, and to my delight, no one sat next to me. I was relieved to make this last trek to New York without social interaction. I couldn't ever recall being this tired before. It had now been seventeen hours of flying and waiting. The trip to New York was another eight hours. We took off smoothly and I dozed off almost immediately.

A polite SAS flight attendant awakened me a few hours later, asking if I would like something to drink. The tall blond-haired man across the aisle was sipping on what smelled like a beer. I noticed the stewardess had an assortment of all sorts of drinks on her cart. I had been taught that beer was *haram* (forbidden) in Islam, even though when I was about ten, Abboo had given me my first sip of Pakistani-brewed beer in the Lahore *gymkhana*. I remember it tasting bitter, but nice.

Abboo also kept whiskey in his closet in Lahore for when we would entertain American executives visiting from GE. Nevertheless, Abboo was a very prudent and self-controlled man. That same bottle of Johnny Walker had been in his closet for years with the whiskey level barely changing. After we moved to Karachi, both my parents had become increasingly religious. I noticed this trend in Ammi much more than Abboo. Eventually, the whiskey bottle vanished, and alcohol was tagged as *haram*. I was to stay as far away from it as possible.

I politely asked the flight attendant for a Coke.

As I sipped my drink, my thoughts again turned to Karachi. In many ways, Karachi was the antithesis of Lahore. While on the outside, life in Lahore presented the façade of a tranquil and peaceful existence, there was absolutely nothing tranquil about Karachi. It was a bustling seaport of over fifteen million people. The locals stayed up until the wee hours of the morning enjoying food, festivities, sports, drugs, and the occasional AK-47 skirmish. Wedding parties would kick-off around ten at night and go on until three in the morning. Ethnic, political, and economic tensions were never far from boiling over in Karachi.

Yet Karachi had a charm of its own. One simply had to be street-smart enough to explore it in the right way. And, at only twelve years old, I did just that. The key, I learned, was not to die before your street IQ reached the survival point.

As I thought about Karachi, my thoughts immediately turned to my best friend, Jamaluddin, or Jamal as I affectionately called him. I missed him already. There had been a long line of friends waiting outside my gate to bid me farewell, but none looked as gloomy as Jamal. Still, it was hard not to smile as I recalled our very first meeting.

My parents and I had recently moved from Lahore. I had no friends. We moved into a new bungalow where I would live until leaving for the United States. I remember seeing a big, beautiful, blue-and-red striped kite about 300 feet in the air and immediately made a beeline for the street to chase after it.

This was a common scene on the streets of Karachi—kids running after a kite whose string had been skillfully cut by another flyer, the errant kite sailing away from its former owner. Kite flying is serious business in Pakistan and is not to be confused with its American counterpart, where smooth nylon string is attached to a plastic kite flying thirty feet in the air while the family applauds. In Pakistan, kite string is called *manja* and is covered by a shredded glass paste which, if you are careless, can do some serious damage to your fingers. However, in the hands of a skilled kite flyer, the *manja* is a weapon meant to bring embarrassment to all other kite flyers.

A kite in the air is a target for another flyer. To cut its string, the other flyer slashes his own kite across it in mid-air, and just like that, you have an ownerless kite, which is now fair game for every child, and even some adults, to chase and recover. Annually, many children die in Karachi chasing kites, either by being hit by a car or by falling through an open manhole.

Fortunately, on that breezy autumn day, I was able to trace that blue-and-red object of beauty to the park across from my home and the only thing standing between me and bragging rights was a fair-skinned boy with chestnut brown hair. He was a shade taller than I and cursing a blue streak as he laughed out loud. We both caught the string at the same time. He continued his impressive cursing and hinted that bad things were about to happen to me if I did not let go. Being the new kid on the block, I thought it wise to let go of the string. But Jamal fascinated me.

He was dressed in the native *shalwar-kamiz*, a loose-fitting outfit that many locals wear. He smiled and shook my hand and introduced himself. I did the same.

"Do you play cricket?" he asked.

I nodded. Cricket was my favorite sport. He invited me to come to his street to play that evening.

In Karachi, all you need to start a game of cricket is a piece of board to serve as the *wicket* (our version of a strike zone), a tennis ball, a bat, and a few boys. Cars respect this obstruction in the street and slowly navigate around the activity. It didn't take long for Jamal and me to become bosom buddies. He was an outstanding batsman, and I, a bowler.

Jamal's family, like mine, was *Mahajir*—a term referring to those of us whose families immigrated to the newly-independent Pakistan in 1947. Those who wanted to leave the rule of Great Britain and live in a Muslim nation left India and moved north. They hoped to enjoy the brotherhood that supposedly exists in Islam. Ironically, those Muslims who were already living in the provinces that became Pakistan were not so welcoming of the *Mahajirs*. This was the beginning of a long-standing feud between the many ethnic sects of Karachi.

It wouldn't be until much later in our youth that both Jamal and I would start to realize the seismic impact of such seeds of hate, how it corroded our city and how manipulative political forces would harness it for their own ends. At this stage, we only cared about flying and chasing kites, batting and bowling, eating *aloo-cholay* (our favorite spicy potato and chick-pea delicacy) and drinking an amazing new bottled drink from the US called *Coca-Cola*.

Life was simple, and it was great to have a friend with whom to explore Karachi.

Only six hours to go before reaching New York. I had a short layover before heading to my final destination: Dallas, Texas. I wondered why New York was called the Big Apple and I also wondered if I would see many cowboys in Texas.

In addition to my obsession with *Archie Comics*, my only other frame of reference for America had come from watching syndicated television shows such as *CHiPs* and *The Six Million Dollar Man*. Those programs portrayed a positive picture of good guys stopping bad guys. In Karachi, the phrase *honest cop*, was an oxymoron.

Another program, *The Mary Tyler Moore Show*, depicted a woman far different than the conservative Pakistani girls I encountered. Girls were often viewed as a burden to their parents, thanks to the dowry-driven, male-dominated culture of Pakistan.

Then there was the show named after the city I was headed to: *Dallas*. As far as I knew, most Americans in Texas were wealthy and owned oil wells. They had promiscuous wives with big hair, horses, and wore cowboy hats and boots. I was entirely unsure how a five-foot-nine, skinny, brown-skinned, black-haired kid like me was going to fit in.

But I was determined to find out.

Lunch was being served on the plane now and I was fascinated by how different the food was starting to look and feel. Everything was so nicely wrapped and segregated. There were separate packages for cheese, crackers, sandwich, mustard, sugar, and creamer.

I took my time unwrapping everything while I observed the state of the cabin. The passengers, especially those who joined us in Dubai, looked disheveled. I made a note to comb my hair prior to disembarking in New York. Even though I had the visa stamped in my passport, I had heard of horror stories from my cousins of US immigration officers conducting inquisitions of young men travelling from foreign countries into America. I had to make a good impression.

Thinking of my passport caused me to instinctively check for the brown leather attaché that Abboo had purchased for me to secure all my travel documents. In it were my passport, some American currency, important phone numbers and addresses of relatives in the US, and the all-important *acceptance letter*.

If the US visa stamp is akin to the Constitution for an international student, then the acceptance letter from the university is like the Declaration of Independence in terms of its importance. It is the formal communiqué from a US university confirming the student's acceptance into the institution. I read mine in disbelief for what must have been the zillionth time. "The University of Texas is pleased to inform you of your acceptance into the Computer Science and Engineering program."

As I read the word engineering, I felt an emptiness in the pit of my stomach. I wasn't at all keen about the math awaiting me as an engineering student. My grades in college, which is eleventh and twelfth grade in Pakistan, were not good enough to get into one of the only two engineering universities in Karachi. Of course, to earn good grades, you must attend classes. I spent much of my time in what they called the common room, playing table tennis. Not making class attendance mandatory for a fifteen-year-old was not a wise policy, but that's how college worked in Pakistan.

I wasn't even sure that I wanted to be an engineer. But in the early eighties, all white-collar, upper-middle class kids in Pakistan were given two choices for their careers. You were either technical (engineering-bound) or you were medical and tagged as destined for medical greatness. Only kids with poor grades or bad attitudes were shoved into commerce, which meant they were good for nothing but business. It is more than a little ironic that those future businessmen would be the ones hiring the engineers and doctors. However, no one asked me for my opinion and logic has nothing to do with such matters in Pakistan. I was admitted into the prestigious, all boys, BVS High School in Karachi. And since I had better grades in math than biology, at the age of twelve, I was encouraged to choose the technical route and focus on engineering. Besides, Abboo had been setting the expectation for me all along that I would one day go to the States. I had several cousins in Texas, and the choice was quickly narrowed down to that state.

Next, I had to go through the grueling process of preparing for the SAT. I had to score at a certain level and, because of a tight deadline for getting my visa, I would have only one shot at the test. I memorized long words like *pugnacious* and *ostentatious*. Did people talk that way in America? Officer Ponch in *CHiPs* certainly didn't. And he was the law. And J.R. sure used a bunch of strange words in *Dallas*, but you would never find them on the SAT. And he was a millionaire.

I was so nervous, Abboo gave me Valium so I could sleep the night before the big exam. The stakes were high, and I knew it. Somehow, I scrounged out a score high enough to be accepted. I also had to pass the TOEFL exam (Test of English as a Foreign Language). No problem. All those comic books were good enough to carry me through that exam.

I knew the odds were against me, but I had an uncanny feeling that I was destined to go to the United States of America. Something was drawing me toward this adventure. I felt that it was a time for new beginnings, a turning of a fresh page in life. A new birth.

I finished my lunch and the polite, blonde SAS flight attendant collected my tray, asking if I wanted anything more to drink. I smiled thinking that Abboo wasn't there to monitor my sugar intake. Besides, I needed to kill another four hours. "Another Coca-Cola, please."

As I gazed at the beautiful clouds outside my window, my thoughts drifted back to the journey of growing up in Karachi that brought me to this point. Unlike Lahore, where I had no family, Karachi was packed with aunts, uncles, and many cousins. Most of my grandparents had passed on early, but Dadi Ma, my grandmother on Abboo's side, lived with us. She was in her mid-eighties but still good for a game of cards.

I had a particularly close relationship with my Uncle Imran. He was Ammi's brother, and he lived only a few blocks away, with my Aunt Zarina and my three cousins. Uncle Imran was Abboo's opposite. While my father was a quiet man, my uncle was loud and funny, always ready with a joke. He was a prankster. My father was a white-collar businessman while my uncle worked in a factory. Abboo was conservative when it came to risk-taking, whether with his investments or with me. Uncle Imran was the one I would run to if I wanted to learn how to ride a motorbike. He always treated me special and we had an uncle-nephew bond that I treasured.

His wife, my Aunt Zarina, was more guarded. There was an inexplicable tension in our interactions that I couldn't quite comprehend. Perhaps it was the close relationship I had with my cousin, Natasha. She was an attractive girl, only a few years younger than me, and we were close. In Pakistani culture, it is perfectly acceptable for cousins to be married. However, as Natasha and I grew older, I noticed my aunt deliberately trying to create distance between us.

Although dating in Karachi was not unheard of for the rich, Pakistan was, and still is, primarily an arranged-marriage culture. For upper-middle-class families like ours, the story went something like this: if you went to a party or a wedding and saw—and hopefully interacted with—a girl you liked, then you would talk to your mother. She then would consult with your father and the family matchmaker.

Every family has at least one matchmaker, generally a well-connected aunt or elder female. The matchmaker assesses the situation, obtains the credentials of the girl's family, and then, if all systems are a go, she lobs an initial feeler to the other side. If it is well-received, then the proceedings move rapidly through the meet-and-greet phase where the boy is usually invited to visit the girl's home.

During the visit, the girl, usually adorned in a pretty outfit plus a *dupata* to cover her head, joins the group at an appropriate time, bringing something sweet to eat and drink. A brief Q&A may ensue for the boy to explain how he will provide for her. This is more a formality at this point.

Depending on the families' status in society, the boy and girl might talk alone further, go out for a cup of coffee, or get to know each other better over the course of several meetings. Any prolonged dating, holding of hands, or kissing was prohibited, so boys made up their minds almost exclusively based on the girl's appearance.

Matchmakers put extreme value on arranging for girls to be engaged early, usually by age nineteen or twenty. Twenty-five was considered ancient. While I wasn't sure that I wanted to be engaged to anyone at a young age, I wasn't certain that Natasha desired the same. However, all of that changed tragically.

About five years after we moved to Karachi, a terrible event happened. It was 1984, a turbulent time in both Pakistan and Afghanistan. The Soviet offensive against Afghanistan and the valiant insurrection by the Mujahideen—backed by the United States—was in full swing. Because of the Soviet-Afghan conflict, Afghan refugees moved into Pakistan in hordes.

At that time, Pakistan was being run by General Zia-ul-Haq, who dealt with his political rivals in a brutal fashion. He crushed the socialist democracy uprising led by Benazir Bhutto, the thirty-one-year-old daughter of the former Prime Minister Zulfikar Ali Bhutto.[9] In Pakistani politics, political figures often re-emerge, sometimes personally, and at other times, through their offspring.

All the havoc led to riots and the imposition of curfews in Karachi. People only had certain windows of time in which to get to and from work. On one of these curfew-controlled summer evenings, Uncle Imran was leaving his plant on his motorcycle. That morning, in a rush to get to work, he had forgotten his helmet. Sadly, that turned out to be a fatal mistake.

As he sped through a roundabout on his way home, a water tanker in a similar hurry collided with the rear end of Imran's small Honda 150 CC bike. Uncle Imran's head hit the concrete and he died instantly. He was only forty-five years old.

Initially, I was told that my uncle had been in an accident and Ammi and my aunt had rushed to the hospital. I was instructed to stay with my cousins, but it didn't take me long to sense that something was terribly wrong. The reactions and stares of my neighbors as I walked to my uncle's home, the whispers, the unusually long and teary-eyed hug with Mohammed, the shopkeeper next door and one of uncle's best friends, all hung over me like a cloud of doom.

When a tragedy occurs in Pakistani culture, crowds gather quickly. No one in the crowd outside my uncle's house was smiling. My worst fears were confirmed within the hour when our car slowly pulled up to the door. Ammi rushed my aunt, who was wailing, out of the car and into the house. I will never forget the look Ammi gave me as she passed by. She looked unusually calm. A slight nod of her head said it all. Uncle Imran was gone.

I remember the intense sense of loss I felt. But what was odd was how others reacted to me. I couldn't put my finger on exactly what it was, but it was different than the normal reaction to a child who had lost his uncle.

I would understand completely in about four months.

That summer of 1984 felt like the longest summer of my young life. Natasha acted like a completely different person after her father's death and didn't cry for a whole week. She walked around in a daze before finally breaking down. As was customary, my aunt went into seclusion for four months and ten days and could not be around any males or leave the house unless absolutely necessary.

Natasha cooked, cleaned, and watched over Zain and Seema, her two younger siblings. But there was a distance between us, and I couldn't help feeling that it wasn't her father's death that was creating it. It was as if she knew something but couldn't express it.

I missed my uncle too, and poured myself into cricket, field hockey, table tennis, and any other sport I could find. I discovered that I was proficient at these. Jamal and I spent hours playing our own version of cricket in my garage. Several times a month, Ammi would take me to the graveyard where her parents, other relatives, and now Uncle Imran were buried. Each had a marble tombstone with dates and the occasional noble epitaph. I did not want to be there while my mother would go from grave to grave, lighting incense, and reading from her ancient green prayer book. I never read the tombstones.

There were two welcome distractions that summer. The first was a brand new, white Mazda 323 sedan that Abboo brought home one day. It was the company's car, but I was unaware of this. My father's privacy extended to his financial life, so I never knew that the company paid for almost everything. To those outside our family, such as my friend Jamal, we appeared wealthy. The reality was quite different.

My second distraction was a growing passion for pop music and my new Sony Walkman. After the release date of a major album, it took only a few months for hit songs to be copied on cassette tapes and then black-marketed from Bangkok to Bombay and everywhere in between. All of us English-speaking, *gymkhana*-member Karachi teenagers were busy listening to Michael Jackson's *Thriller* and learning how to moonwalk, while keeping a close eye on the rising ethnic and political tensions in our city.

Finally, it grew cooler as fall arrived and school was back in session. Now in eleventh grade, I rode with Abboo in the mornings to DJ College, which was only fifteen minutes from his office. This was a special time, and the highlight for me was learning how to change gears in our little Suzuki minivan. In Pakistan, the driver sits on the right. Abboo would press the clutch and I would shift gears with my right hand.

I had an up-and-down relationship with Abboo. Perhaps that is true of most teenage boys, but what was unique to him was how he would shut down when conflict between us proved to be overwhelming to him. He would stop talking to me for days. One of the primary sources of conflict had to deal with night cricket.

A major fad in Karachi was playing cricket tournaments under the lights. These would go on until four or five in the morning, depending on how successful your team was in the tournament. One night, I remember creating a fake lump in my bed and sneaking out through the first-floor balcony room that led to the alley. When I returned at around four AM, Ammi was saying her prayers in that room and gestured to me to come in through the master bedroom door where Abboo was sleeping.

I knew it was going to be bad. Most fathers would have the paddle ready, but not Abboo. He simply opened the door and went back to bed without saying a single word. I remember apologizing profusely and begging him to speak to me. Not a word. It took a week before things returned to normal.

It had been only four months since my uncle died, but it felt like a long time had passed. Natasha, my aunt Zarina, and my cousins were slowly picking up the pieces of their lives and moving forward. We resumed going to Bandu Khan's, our favorite barbecue place, with them.

Things were just starting to feel normal again when it happened. I had a new neighbor, a boy named Saleem. He had moved with his family from the Middle East to Karachi a few months back. Saleem was fifteen, pudgy, and a bit quirky— always bragging about his former school, friends, athletic accomplishments, and such. In addition, he couldn't keep a secret to save his life. Some of us wished badly that he would go back to Kuwait.

It was around eleven at night and we had all just arrived from a night cricket match, because our team had been eliminated early. We were standing under the streetlamp outside my home when Saleem came bursting out of his gate. Even in the shadows, I could see a gleam in his eyes.

He walked straight up to me and gently put his right arm around my neck, as boys often do in our culture. Pulling me aside, he whispered that he had over-heard a big secret about me. Try as he might to contain his excitement, his whisper was still not low enough to keep Jamal from overhearing.

Jamal, standing about ten feet away, shot Saleem a strange glare.

Not to be deterred, Saleem unloaded what he had overheard Mrs. Anwar, our town gossip, share with his mother over *chai* just hours before. "You are not your parents' boy," he blurted.

"What are you talking about? Of course I am!" I responded, feeling a knot forming in my stomach.

Saleem grinned, obviously enjoying himself. Jamal was now mouthing things to him, his face furious.

"No, no, you are actually your uncle's son, man. The one that got killed." Those words hit me like a runaway truck.

Somehow, I had known. I had always known. All the occasional slip-ups by family acquaintances over the years. Slip-ups I had corrected. All the wink-wink by my older cousins who seemed to be in on a joke. It all started to make sense.

As I stood there dumbfounded, Saleem went on to tell me that Ammi and Abboo couldn't have children and that my biological father, Imran, had chosen to let me be raised by his sister. I suddenly felt sick as I thought of Zarina being my mother and Natasha my sister. No wonder they wanted to keep us at a distance.

But why didn't I feel a bond with Zarina? Uncle Imran being my father totally resonated with me, but not her being my mother. I took Saleem aside, away from everyone since by now it was evident to my friends that the cat was out of the bag, a cat they had all conspired to protect for so many years. I wondered for how long. Anger rose inside me.

"So, Zarina then..." My voice trailed off.

"Not your mother." Saleem answered.

"What?" My head was spinning. I rested my hand against a tree.

"I think it was another aunt. She's dead too."

I grabbed Saleem's collar with both hands. "You are lying!" I screamed.

But deep down I didn't believe that he was. I knew that there was no way for him to know all of this unless it was true. And, as obnoxious as Saleem could be sometimes, even he had to know that this would be a very bad practical joke. I turned and ran toward my house. I had to know the truth. And there was only one person I knew who could explain all of this to me.

Sometimes, to keep warm, Ammi would sleep in my room, since it was an interior room. I woke her up, tears running down my cheeks. I repeated what I'd been told. At first, she told me to just go to sleep and not believe any of it. But when I wouldn't go to bed, she relented.

"What does your heart tell you?" she asked.

"That I am yours and Abboo's son." I stammered.

Saleem had given me too much information for her to dodge my inquisition. When I persisted, she calmly got up, walked to a closet, and returned with a photo album. There in front of me were wedding pictures of Uncle Imran and a beautiful young woman. She looked familiar. She looked like me. And then it hit me. Her name was Alina. She was Ammi's first cousin on her father's side. Ammi explained that Alina had tragically died giving birth to me.

Uncle Imran wanted to marry Zarina, but she was not ready for marriage. Alina, due to advanced polio, was not expected to live very long. My uncle—my biological father—heroically proposed to Alina despite the likelihood of losing her. They enjoyed a wonderful honeymoon in London. In fact, she was so happy, according to Ammi, that she even joked with my parents, telling them she would will them her firstborn. She knew that they could not have children.

When Alina's pregnancy was confirmed, doctors told her she faced serious risks to her life if she gave birth to a child, and that abortion was the safest choice to protect her own life. Alina would hear none of it. Although on the outside she seemed fragile, Alina possessed an indomitable spirit. As the time approached, not only did she make Imran promise that there would be no choosing her life over the baby's in case she was incapacitated during labor, she also made him promise that the baby would go to Ammi and Abboo if her life were to end.

He agreed.

On August 20, 1967, Alina departed from this world due to complications during childbirth. In the end, it wasn't the polio, but too much anesthesia that killed her. However, at twenty-three, she brought a new, polio-free life into this world, filled the bosom of her childless cousin, and saved her beloved husband from having to raise a baby on his own. If I had only paid attention to those tombstones at the graveyard, I would have noticed the one that Ammi always took me to. The one where we lingered. If I had only bothered to glance up, I would have read: "Alina Sharif, 23, wife of Imran Sharif."

Her death date was my birthday.

I felt angry, sad, and distrustful as my mind tried to process the information that had been forced on me. Overwhelmed, I cried much of the night. By dawn the next morning, I left for a long walk with my cricket bat in hand. Thirty minutes into my walk, and much to my surprise, a new emotion started to take hold of me: gratitude.

I was grateful for the clear hand of Providence. God spared my life and allowed me to discover this truth after the passing of both my birth parents. I couldn't imagine how I would have felt if one or both were still alive. I felt grateful that my birth mother, Alina, had the courage to do what she did. I was thankful that I never contracted polio, which Ammi told me had surprised the medical staff involved in my birth.

Most of all, my thoughts were about Abboo. Ammi had shared that he was very worried that once I found out, I would no longer love him. It became clear to me that although the words *mother* and *father* have biological significance, they are also terms of endearment we award to those who love us like that.

Despite his passivity, Abboo loved me dearly. He was not going to lose his son. And, to this day, although each is aware that the other knows the truth, we've never needed to discuss the matter. On my way home, I felt at peace. I ran into Jamal who had a cricket ball in his hand. We instinctively started to play. He would bowl to me. I would gently tap the ball back to him with my bat. There was something cathartic about that.

"So?" I asked. "You knew?"

Jamal nodded, his eyes staring at the concrete. "The whole city knew," he added.

I flinched at the comment but managed a smile.

"Ammi?" I inquired as I looked into his genuinely concerned brown eyes.

He nodded again.

"Yes, she forbade us from saying anything. 'All in good time,' she said."

I thought of the graveyard trips and the grave. Perhaps it was her way of hoping to introduce the subject. I am sure she thought, someday he will notice and then we can have this uncomfortable discussion.

It was our culture.

"You playin' in the tournament this weekend?" I asked with a smile, noticing the worry dissipating from Jamal's face as he smiled back in relief.

"Only if you are," he replied.

And that was that. A new chapter started.

I was suddenly jolted back to reality by the voice of our captain announcing our descent to New York City. As I wiped an unexpected tear from my cheek, he explained that the lucky ones sitting on the left side of the plane would get a fabulous view of the famous Statue of Liberty. That was my side, so I braced myself for a good view.

My two moms

They also started playing a movie about New York welcoming the world. And there it was, the most amazing of sights. The movie described the Statue as a centennial gift given by France to the United States in 1886[10] as a symbol of friendship. It was one of the first sights that immigrants saw many years ago as they disembarked from ships into New York. And more importantly, it was what Lady Liberty represented that intrigued me the most: freedom.

It seemed that America stood welcoming those whom the world rejects, inviting me, the immigrant, to come and enter through its golden door.

The movie flashed a close-up of those powerful words engraved on the pedestal upon which the Statue rests:

"Give me your tired, your poor, Your huddled masses yearning to breathe free, The wretched refuse of your teeming shore, Send these, the homeless, tempest-tost, to me, I lift my lamp beside the golden door!"

I wondered how many immigrants had experienced the same feeling that I was, a combination of excitement and sheer terror. The excitement part was winning now. Who wouldn't be inspired by such an invitation?

What was not wasted on me then and isn't to this day, is that the focus was not on the rich or the powerful but on the meek. It seemed that America stood welcoming those whom the world rejects, inviting me, the immigrant, to come and enter through its golden door.

As the wheels of the Airbus finally touched down at New York's John F. Kennedy Airport, I smiled and wondered what lay beyond the golden door for me.

PART II

What a Country!

Chapter 3

ℰTHE ENTRY

New York, New York, is everything they say.
And no place that I'd rather be.
Where else can you do a half a million things?
All at a quarter to three.[11]

ℰt was almost a quarter to three and Huey Lewis couldn't have been more accurate in his description. I was amazed to see so much hustle and bustle at the JFK airport as Mr. Khan and I scurried out of the airplane and made our way to the immigration lines. My heart beat with excitement. I checked my documents for the umpteenth time as we got in the customs and border control line. I immediately noticed the efficiency with which the line was moving. For starters, there *was* a line. In Pakistan, a line is a mere suggestion.

The tall, white immigration officer, dressed in a dark blue uniform, was professional and polite. "Going off to Texas, huh?" he asked with a smile.

I relaxed. *Surely Cousin Aslam was exaggerating about the ratio of Pakistani students who get sent right back at border control.*

"Yes sir. Going to school."

"How long is your stay in New York?" he probed as he scanned all the visa stamps and the precious admissions document from the university.

Just stick to the point. Stay on message. "Just for the day," I replied.

Stamp…bang…stamp. Few sounds are more melodious for an immigrant entering a US airport than those one hears from an immigration officer as he waves you in.

Mr. Khan and I collected our bags and came out of the airport. His sons were there to greet us. Both wore cool college sweatshirts and seemed well-adjusted to the States. I felt a bit shy and insecure around them. I handed them my bags and piled into their station wagon, which came complete with faux-wood paneling.

Looking back, thirty years removed, it's strange the little things one remembers about the most memorable days of one's short life. I remember how clean their car smelled compared to Pakistani cars and that the radio was playing *One Night Love Affair* by the Canadian crooner, Bryan Adams. I took it all in.

My connection was from LaGuardia airport, and Mr. Khan's son Khalid insisted on taking me there. I wasn't about to argue. I was too engrossed in people-watching. Everyone seemed so tall. And there were the yellow cabs that I saw on *Taxi*, the T.V. show. People were jumping in and out of them.

I noticed the diversity of attire. Suits, shorts, jeans, brightly-colored tank tops, t-shirts, and men wearing black skull-caps. Being from a Muslim country, I had never seen anyone who was Jewish before. As in Europe, I was amazed by the clothing girls wore—presenting far too much information in the way they dressed. Mind you, I was hardly a saint (or *Imam*, I should say), and I certainly didn't object.

My head was spinning as we drove toward Queens, where LaGuardia was located, especially with all the cars driving the wrong way on the road. And it was not wasted on me that we were driving on the Grand Central Parkway. Why on earth did they name it a parkway, I wondered? Shouldn't one park on a parkway?

We stopped for gas and I came face-to-face with my first vending machine sporting a bright red *Coca-Cola* logo on it. My dear Aunt Razia had given me one of the most practical gifts one can give a young student coming to the States: a roll of quarters. The vending machine sported the message, "Insert 25 cents." I put in a quarter and waited. Nothing happened. I was wondering when the server would bring me my Coke, but then heard Khalid and his brother Asif howling with laughter.

"Push," they said. "Just push the dang thing."

I turned red, understanding the flaw in my thinking. Down came the refreshing Coke with the simple push of a button. It tasted wonderful.

As we made our way through the traffic, I took in the breathtaking New York City skyline, something I had only seen in postcards. It looked like a massive jungle of buildings, both old and new, and seemed to possess an untamable power. My later years in America would take me to the heart of midtown time and time again, and I would grow to love this city.

One of the highlights of my journey to LaGuardia was a stop at McDonald's. Neither Mr. Khan nor his two boys were committed to eating *halal*, so they introduced me to my first-ever Quarter Pounder with Cheese and those delicious french fries. Oh, my goodness. I could see why kids didn't want to leave this place. What with a playground, music, birthday parties, and Happy Meals, it seemed quintessentially American. Little did I know at the time how significant a role this place would play in my future life.

If these people love dogs this much, how much more do they value people?

We arrived at LaGuardia, said quick goodbyes, and I boarded my flight to Dallas. After thirty-four hours of travel, I was beyond exhausted. A sweet, affluent older couple from Grapevine, Texas, sat next to me. I noticed in them a different accent and a level of friendliness that contrasted with the edgy nature of the New Yorkers. They spoke about their "boy" back home and the husband pulled out a picture from his wallet to show me a picture of their Great Dane. I was amazed by the level of endearment that a dog, something that is *najees* or unclean in Islamic culture, could have in an American home.

If these people love dogs this much, how much more do they value people?

Three and a half hours later we finally landed in Dallas, where I was greeted by my cousin Aslam and his family.

My first words? "I want to sleep."

I woke up in the most comfortable bed I had ever slept in. I didn't even recall getting into it. It was now around two in the afternoon, and I had slept for fourteen hours straight.

Cousin Aslam was an older cousin with a master's degree in engineering from Penn State and another master's in computer science from the University of Texas. He was the prototypical male relative my parents wanted me to emulate. In their minds, he had things figured out. As it turned out, this was true in *his* mind as well.

Aslam was full of all kinds of wisdom on life in America and eager to take me under his wing. He and his wife, Sameera, whom I called *Bhabi* (sister), lived in Plano, Texas, about forty-five minutes from my ultimate destination, Arlington, where the university was located. I called him *Aslam Bhai*. *Bhai*, or brother, was how all cousins in Indo-Pak culture are referred. Unlike in the US, there isn't much of a leap between your true siblings and your first or second cousins.

All my older cousins viewed it their responsibility to ensure that I followed "the path"—educational, economic, and spiritual—correctly and responsibly.

Aslam had a clear vision for me, which he shared in short order. I was to go to school, study computer science (like him), make straight As (like him), find a job, earn my master's, and get married to an educated Muslim girl in the States. Then both of us would work, but we'd live off my income and pay off the mortgage with her income. I was somewhat afraid of Cousin Aslam. Sameera Bhabi, on the other hand, was sweet and fit the traditional Pakistani mold of the older brother's wife who lets you get away with things and cooks your favorite dishes.

Plano is a beachhead for many Pakistani immigrant families in the Dallas-Fort Worth area. I was fascinated by how many friends and extended family lived cocoon-like existences in America. They watched Pakistani television via satellite dish. They ate Pakistani food bought from the Indo-Pak supermarket that proudly advertised *halal* everything. In some ways, I found this comforting. I could find the same mango chutney here that I loved back home. But in other ways, there was something incongruous about it all. I wanted to experience this new culture and world, and I couldn't wait to have the opportunity to meet my host, Nazneen, in Arlington later that week.

I began to appreciate how hard a person must strive to make it in America. But I also noticed that…hard work afforded…a very comfortable and independent lifestyle.

Nazneen was my uncle's daughter on Abboo's side. She was about twelve years older than me, and as a term of endearment I called her *Apa* (older sister). In many ways, she too, was a trailblazer like my mother. One of the only girls from our family to come to the States to study, she was a single girl working on-campus as a teacher's assistant and at the university bookstore, living in her own apartment, and was the president of the Pakistani Student Association at UT Arlington. She was also about to graduate with a Chemistry degree. She stood about five-feet-six inches tall and had a broad smile. I thanked Aslam Bhai and Sameera Bhabi, and we were off to my new temporary home (Nazneen's apartment) until the summer semester began in three weeks.

Spending time with Nazneen was refreshing. I quickly observed that there were different shades of cultural assimilation into America, and Nazneen was more westernized. She had a wide range of white, black, and Pakistani friends. She also dressed more western than most Pakistani immigrants but had her boundaries. She worked long, odd hours at her two jobs and would leave by 6:00 a.m. to open the chem lab or do inventory and then go to her classes until late evening. I began to appreciate how hard a person must strive to make it in America. But I also noticed that her hard work afforded her a very comfortable and independent lifestyle. That part I liked very much.

My first few days at Nazneen's apartment were novel. I loved her apartment complex—Brookhaven Apartments—such a pleasant western name. It had its own pool. The summer heat in Texas certainly did not make me homesick. The auto dealership right across from the apartment complex sold Camaros, and I was awed by those gorgeous cars and the bright colors. Everything seemed amazing.

And then it hit me: unstoppable bouts of deep anxiety, homesickness, and sheer panic about the unknowns that lay before me. I don't know if it was the news Nazneen gave me earlier about the tripling of the international student rates per credit hour, or if it was being alone in the apartment all day long waiting for her to return. Maybe in a strange way, watching *General Hospital* and *Days of Our Lives*, the two leading daytime soap operas, took its toll. Everyone I saw on those two shows was rich, beautiful, and had relationships: Frisco and Felicia, Robert and Anna, and Luke and Laura. I was nothing like them. And sitting here, eight thousand miles away from home, alone all day with barely enough money to pay for one semester's-worth of tuition, no job, no cool clothes, no car, and no girl, it seemed a forlorn existence. Time was crawling.

I tried calling home to see if that would bring any solace. After asking permission from Nazneen Apa, I dialed a long code into the phone. Calling Karachi from Arlington cost $1.30 a minute in those days, and there was more than a 50 percent chance you would hear the dreaded all-circuits-are-busy message. Even the dial tone sounded like it came from a million miles away. It only made me feel farther away from home. I finally got Ammi on the line. Her voice sounded faint and hollow over the bad phone line. I told her that I loved her.

"Jamal keeps coming over," she said. "He just sits in our living room and cries."

The thought of my best pal missing me like that both saddened me and warmed my heart. His family didn't have a phone, so calling him was not an option. Understanding that this four-minute phone call was costing me what most people would earn for two days of labor in Pakistan, I ended the call feeling even emptier than before.

Later that afternoon, I walked outside and saw cars whooshing by. Everyone seemed to have a purpose but me. No amount of *Archie Comics* could prepare me for what I was experiencing—full-blown culture shock.

The summer semester finally arrived. Nazneen took me to the University of Texas at Arlington to register and I was awed by the campus. It was one thing to see pictures in a catalog, but walking the hallways gave me goosebumps all over.

In the mid-eighties, UT Arlington (UTA) had already built a solid reputation as a strong engineering, business, and nursing school. As a result, many international students from Pakistan attended there. People in Karachi jokingly called UTA, "UPA," the University of Pakistan at Arlington. So I was pleasantly surprised when I ran into Raees, one of my high-school acquaintances, in the university post-office. The big world I had been stressing about just became a bit smaller.

My world soon became smaller still. Raees introduced me to several of his roommates, one of whom cherished the sport of table-tennis almost as much as I did. I thought *ping-pong* was a degrading term for this beloved sport. The difference between the two is that in table tennis, you break a sweat.

While UTA was primarily a commuter school back then, they did have some dormitories, and I was expected to stay in them for the summer. As luck would have it, I wasn't the only male student getting a head start by attending summer school. There were so many, UTA ran out of room in the men's dormitory. Nine lucky men and I were assigned to the Lipscomb dormitory—the girl's dorm.

I wanted to break out like the Russian comedian, Yakov Smirnoff, by screaming out, "Whaaat a country!"

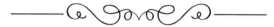

One of the young men who also had the good fortune of living in the girls'
dorm was my dormmate, Joe. Joseph Frederick Jackson was the first black man I'd
ever met. Prior to that, I had either seen black people on TV boxing (Mohammed
Ali), running (Carl Lewis), singing (Michael Jackson), or committing crimes and
being chased down by Officer Ponch on *CHiPs*. In general, the narrow image portrayed to me was that blacks were either very athletic, talented, or not productive
members of society. There was no middle ground.

Joe was none of those things. He was of medium build, maybe an inch taller
than me, and a communications major. Meeting someone who was not a computer science or electrical engineering major was a rare treat. In the mid-eighties, it
seemed that all international students arriving in the US from Asia swore a secret
oath to major only in those two categories. In Pakistan, most students that didn't
specialize in computers, engineering, or medicine wound up as rickshaw drivers.

"You can make a living with that?" I asked.

"Sure, man." Joe replied as he gave me a strange handshake, curling his fingers
into mine and then giving it a tug. "We got all kinds of majors 'round here. Wait
till you take old man Thompson for 'Diffy-q. Oooooh, sweet Jesus. You be getting
yo' butt to communications in a hurry, boy."

I hoped I'd gotten the gist of what he'd just said, and I made a mental note
to ask Raees if there were any options other than Dr. Thompson for Differential
Equations. Joe was a sophomore and taking some extra summer classes. He was
also in an organization called ROTC and shared that he would be away some
weekends for reserve training. How amazing to get your college degree funded by
the government, I thought. That would never happen in Pakistan.

Joe wore a chain around his neck with a small cross on it. With a biblical
name like Joseph, I assumed that he was a Christian. In Islam, we called him
Yousef and he was a revered prophet who was known for his stunning good looks.

The assumption that Joe was a Christian was reasonable from where I sat,
because in Islam, every man named Mohammed or Ali is Muslim. The names
are straight out of the Quran, our holy book. As a child born in a Muslim home,

you don't become a Muslim. You are born one. So, logically, I assumed every guy named Mark, Luke, or Joseph, would automatically be a Christian based on the biblical origin of their given name. This was, and still is, a view held by most Muslims worldwide.

Joe walked me through the basic protocols of dorm life, and I took it all in. Our room was small with a bed and a desk on either side and no bathroom.

"Nope, we gotta use the one on the north side," Joe said with a grin. Then he added, "Don't make the mistake of walking into the south side one, dude, or Fat Sally will get ya."

"Fat Sally?" I asked, looking confused.

"She's the R.A., man."

"R…A…?" I repeated slowly, still looking puzzled.

Joe looked at me in disbelief, like I was some sort of alien. "Resident Assistant, dude." He then transitioned into what I came to call, Coach Joe mode. "We are gonna have a lot of fun together this summer, Ali," he said, as he left to see his girlfriend.

After he left, panic set in as I realized that I had neglected to ask him if south was to the left or the right. We never used compass points for directions in Pakistan unless we were praying. Then it was always east, facing Mecca.

Yes, janaab *(sir), it will indeed be a summer to remember.*

Classes started in four days and I was scrambling to get the supplies I needed: books, clothes, sneakers and other sundry items. I couldn't believe my political science book alone cost more than what Abboo earned in an entire week. One thing I couldn't survive in America without was an ID. Want to open a college bank account? ID, please. Get a post-office box? ID, please.

I was getting sick and tired of carrying my passport around and having folks constantly mispronounce my name: Owlee, Aaylee, Ollie. Of course my surname, Master, attracted a lot of remarks, too.

Workers could take off their aprons and come out from behind the counter at the end of a shift and order a meal from the same menu that they were cooking just an hour ago.

"That's a cool last name, man." commented the retail clerk at the local grocery store. I found it fascinating that everyday workers were often jovial, even bantering back and forth with customers. I had never witnessed that in Pakistan. In fact, it would be considered inappropriate.

The vibe was completely different with employees in the States. They behaved more like peers and equals with their customers. Workers could take off their aprons and come out from behind the counter at the end of a shift and order a meal from the same menu that they were cooking just an hour ago. And they would be served with a smile. That was radical to me. In Pakistan, people behind the counter do not mingle with those on the other side. It is a different social class. Here, a job was a job.

In order to get my coveted ID, I had been practicing driving on the "wrong" side of the road for several days in Nazneen's nice-smelling car. I was thankful that Abboo had taught me how to change gears in our right-hand-drive minivan in Karachi. Since my passenger seat there was on the left side, it was an easy transition when I practiced in Nazneen's car. I just had to remember not to take an immediate left when I drove out of her apartment complex, something that had already occurred at least once. My dear cousin almost had a conniption in the car, screaming at me to turn back as traffic approached at a distance.

"Relax," I chuckled. "No harm done."

"Just don't do that during the driving test," Nazneen teased.

I enjoyed spending time with my cousin as she showed me the ropes. Finally, I felt I was ready for my big moment and signed up for a driving test. After all, I had been driving on the streets of Karachi for several years back home, which was akin to playing the video game *Galaga* in real life, only with automobiles.

At the DMV, I patiently waited for my turn to take the driving test. Finally, a six-foot-four, stern-looking Texas state trooper, complete with cowboy hat and clipboard, accompanied me to my car. I felt weak at the knees.

He got in the passenger side, and I began driving while he jotted down notes on his clipboard. I resisted the urge to peek. I tried to make small talk, but he didn't seem inclined to chat, so I decided that less was more.

Thanks to my Karachi five-cars-in-three-lanes training, parallel parking was a breeze. As we approached the conclusion of the test, the trooper asked me to put the car in reverse. We were about seventy yards or so from Arlington's busy Cooper Street.

After we rolled back about twenty-five yards or so, he said, "That's good."

Pleased that he liked what I was doing, I continued backing up.

The trooper stared at me strangely and raised his voice an octave. "That's *good*, son."

I matched his stern look with a quizzical one of my own, wondering how long he planned to praise me. But I was determined to get my license, so I kept backing toward Cooper Street as we both noticed cars zipping by.

He yanked the emergency break about ten yards from the street, this time yelling, "STOP!"

"You said it was good," I stammered.

He burst out laughing. "Well, I'll be damned," he said, much to my relief.

Yes, I did get my coveted ID, but it certainly made for an exciting afternoon. English. I thought I knew it.

The semester finally started, and I was excited to go to my first university-level classes in the United States. Chemistry, Introduction to Computer Systems, and Political Science were my first three courses. I was amazed by the amount of structure: tests, assignments, and papers, all planned out with due dates and requirements from the onset. This was very different than in Pakistan, where you could go an entire year before you took the final exam, and then you might not get the results for six months.

The sheer pace of the American collegiate system required far more discipline to succeed than I was accustomed to. Still, I especially enjoyed my chemistry class, and liked my professors and classmates.

I became good friends with one fellow named Sonny, who hailed from Bombay, India. For Pakistanis, it can be challenging to interact with Indians since our nations have fought three wars and are bitter rivals on many fronts. However, since half my family was from India, I always found it easy to connect with Indians.

Both cultures had much in common, and it seemed to me that our governments focused more on the conflicts than the people themselves did. Sonny had a car and we enjoyed driving around Arlington after class.

One evening, Sonny came over to the dorm and we decided to stroll over to the university gym to play some racquetball. As we walked, I put my arm around Sonny's shoulder as a sign of our friendship, a common gesture in the East. Soon, a red Camaro full of guys passed by, honking its horn. I thought it was strange since I didn't see another car anywhere near the Camaro. *Who were they honking at?* A few minutes later a truck drove by, also honking.

At that moment, Sonny and I both almost simultaneously realized the situation. We looked at each other and I gently removed my arm from Sonny's shoulder. I found it interesting how quickly these societal norms start to shape behavior.

Appearing to be openly gay was not without consequence in the 1980s, even in America.

My dormmate, Joe, and I also got to hang out from time to time, but I found it amazing that two people could live in the same room and yet barely see each other. Life was so busy in America, far busier than in the East. Here, everyone was going somewhere, usually in a rush. No one loitered under a streetlamp or on a sidewalk just to chit-chat. Everyone had a schedule to keep. People arrived on time and left on time, whether it was for class, sports, or social events. At times, I longed for the relaxed atmosphere of home, to freely put my arm around my friend Jamal and talk about that day's cricket game or the neighborhood beauty we both fancied, or to go grab a dish of *Aloo-cholay*. But I knew that I had to adjust quickly to this time-oriented society if I wanted to survive.

Joe was off on Fridays and there was no ROTC that weekend.

"Let's go party, man!" he shouted. I smiled a nervous smile, since I didn't fully understand what *party* meant in Joe's vernacular. I liked Joe, but he confused me. The past Sunday morning, he had invited his girlfriend over to our dorm. I recalled our conversation with amusement.

"Hey dude, don't you have pong to play this morning?" he asked, his eyes begging me to say yes.

"It's *table tennis*," I corrected, with a smirk. I was an international student and new to the country, but I wasn't stupid. Certain codes were universal. "So, no church this Sunday?" I asked with large, innocent eyes, as he glared at me with an I'm-gonna-kill-you look.

Shooed off by my roommate, I had wondered how Joe could be a Christian and go to church only on some Sundays, but then on certain other Sundays....

Joe also openly talked about smoking marijuana and other shenanigans. But I was no angel, so that Friday I agreed to tag along with him and several of his buddies to our local bar and grill.

"Let's start you off with something that tastes good. Ever had a piña colada?"

I shook my head. Three drinks later, I was feeling good. My first experience with alcohol was memorable and didn't land me face down in the toilet like it does in the movies. That alcohol was *haram* (forbidden) in Islam did not even occur to me.

Oh well. I will pray twice.

Introduction to Computers was designed to teach students how the university's computer lab works and to help them understand the basics of using a computer. However, the associate professor, Mr. Pitts, had other ideas. He was intent on making us all into professional essay writers by the time the summer ended.

Pitts, a man in his late thirties, balding, with pale white skin, and a wiry build, was undergoing a torture of his own: completing his PhD dissertation. He saw fit to share his pain with his pupils by telling us to research the song "The Sound of Silence" by Simon and Garfunkel and write a thousand-word essay on its meaning—with proper bibliography.

For reasons I couldn't fully comprehend, Pitts seemed to have taken a dislike for me. I had been tardy a few times to the class—still adapting to the whole time-oriented thing—and I made a few lame excuses for turning in some assignments late. But I wasn't prepared for what awaited me in this assignment.

I read the song and did my research. It was an interesting piece of music and I found myself intrigued by the background—the industrial revolution in the sixties—and how it was changing society. I worked diligently on the paper but caught the flu a few days before it was due. I called and left Mr. Pitts a message that I was unable to make it to class and would come to his office to deliver the paper when I had recovered. I never heard back. The next week was finals week and there was no class, so I went and found him in his office, his assistant sitting next to him. He glared at me.

"You are late again."

I explained that I had been battling the flu, but that I had done the paper and the printout date stamp could prove that I had printed it before the deadline.

He snatched the paper from my hand. "Let me see it."

I sat in the corner of his office, my heart beating fast.

A few minutes later, he shook his head. "You didn't write this paper, did you?"

I couldn't believe what I was hearing. "Yes sir, I did," I stammered, a mixture of fear and indignation rising within me.

"No. You didn't. Tell me, Mr. Ali, what's an acoustic ballad?" he asked sarcastically, referring to words I'd used to describe the song in the paper.

"It's when a song doesn't use electronic instruments and relies on other instruments such as the guitar."

He continued quizzing me for a time and I grew more determined with every question as tears started to well up in my eyes. His assistant studied a crack in the floor as this horrifying demonstration of bullying continued. Pitts then scribbled a seventy-five at the top of the paper and almost threw it back at me. I looked at it in shock and disappointment.

"Ali Master, I don't think you have what it takes to make it in the American collegiate system. Maybe it's my self-fulfilling prophesy for you."

I was shaking with anger. The tears couldn't stay inside my eyes. "I wrote the paper," I replied softly. I turned to walk out.

"Come back." he said. He took the paper from my hand once more and changed the grade to an eighty-five. "You either have a bright future in American literature, or you didn't write this paper."

I left and never saw him again after that day. But this was the first time I had experienced prejudice. It was an ugly feeling. Someone without any evidence was convinced that I was not capable of achieving. Why was that? Where did this bias come from? I didn't understand it then and struggle with it to this day. I just know that to some extent we all have it. Some more than others. Some let it show like Pitts and some keep it deep within. What I do know is that we must stamp it out wherever we see it. It was my first experience that contradicted the perfect picture of America I had conjured up in my mind.

Fortunately for me, an eighty-five, combined with my other work in the class, still gave me my first A.

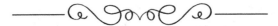

Despite the unnerving experience in Intro to Computers, I was thrilled with how my semester ended. Dr. Whitfield, whom I really liked from my chemistry class, offered me a small scholarship and was very kind to me. It was a much-needed reminder to me that not all white professors despised smart East Asian students.

Sonny and I decided to drive and blow off some steam to celebrate the end of our first-ever US college semester. I asked him to go through the McDonald's drive-through across campus on Abrams Street because I thought the young Hispanic girl that worked the window was really cute, and I was three-for-three this week getting her to flirt with me. Her nametag said "Maria."

"She probably thinks you're Mexican, dude," said Sonny with a cheeky grin. "Wait till she finds out you are a Paki."

"C'mon," I wailed. "Do I really look Mexican?" I said as I glanced at my reflection in the mirror and combed my jet-black mop of hair with my fingers.

"You wish." Sonny laughed.

I gave him a friendly punch on the arm. As the familiar sights of our UT campus faded in the background, I felt a sense of exhilaration. It was nice to have at least some familiar surroundings, a friend or two, and a campus to call home.

Alas, these warm feelings of relief were going to be short-lived.

Chapter 4

CRASH AND BURN

It was the fall of '86. The semester was about to start and the UTA campus had come alive. Rush week was underway, and freshmen were scurrying all over campus. Some looked stressed. Some looked happy. I shook my head and smiled as I saw them waving goodbye to parents who were dropping them off from places like Dallas, a mere forty-five minutes away or even Houston or Oklahoma City, which were only a forty-five-minute plane ride.

It had taken me over thirty hours to arrive in Texas, and it had changed my world completely. One moment I was rich. Now I was poor. One moment I knew the language. Now I was advising other foreign students to watch out when the state trooper praises you. One moment, I could scan the scoreboard on any TV screen and know instantly whether my team was winning or losing the cricket, squash, or field hockey match. Now American-style football was the only game in town. One moment I was tall, dark and handsome (or so I believed). Now I was only dark. I had gone from being normal to being *diverse*.

I was glad I'd been able to ease into the college system by attending summer school. Of course, I was still recovering from my experience with Pitts and was hopeful that he was the exception rather than the rule. Thus far, my experience with other UT instructors and staff validated that Pitts was the exception, as most of my professors seemed genuinely interested in my education and well-being.

One moment I was tall, dark and handsome (or so I believed).
Now I was only dark.

As I heard about and studied the civil rights movement of the sixties, a mere twenty or so years earlier, I was amazed at how much America had progressed in two decades. Good and bad, it was laid out right there in my American history book. In the not-too-distant past, following laws established by duly-elected leaders, people of color weren't allowed to drink from the same water fountain, ride in the front of the bus, or use the same restroom as whites.

I appreciated that the books did not paint a one-sided picture of American history and its leaders. Most intriguing to me about all of this was the potential for change by the leaders and then the citizenry. I was also amazed at how America truly was a nation of laws. The Civil Rights Act of 1964 was a big deal. Immediately after the bill became law, public places and facilities could no longer be segregated. At least on the outside, America literally looked and felt different the day after the passage of this seminal law.[12]

This was unlike the governing process I had witnessed in my homeland. Although it was called a democracy, it felt far more dictatorial. And societal change didn't necessarily follow a major court decision or legislation.

I befriended two other guys at a Pakistan Student Association meeting on campus and we decided to share an apartment, a far more economical arrangement. Assad was a junior and Farhan was a freshman. My dormmate Joe had moved into an apartment with his girlfriend. This was another novel concept that I had never seen before—unmarried men and women living together under the same roof.

Most intriguing to me about all of this was the potential for change by the leaders and then the citizenry.

Assad was of heavy-set build and was the strong silent type. He rode a motorbike and was an Architecture major. He liked his kitchen clean and was the alpha in our apartment. He was from Lahore and a *Punjabi*. *Punjabis* think they own Pakistan, and they run many of its institutions. They frown on *Mohajirs* like me, those whose families migrated from India.

Farhan was tall, skinny, and had curly black hair. He had a great sense of humor and was a fellow Karachiite. I was glad to have Farhan as my roommate, so we could attempt to balance some of Assad's austerity.

Assad and Farhan were a step ahead of me in some ways. They both had jobs at the local McDonald's. I was hoping to get an interview there soon, and Assad, in his usual condescending style, said he would consider putting in a good word for me. He, of course, wanted to see me plead. Assad always had an angle. A day later, he inquired, "So, you'll do dishes this entire week for me?" He laid out the terms he would require for arranging an introduction to the store manager. Of course, he left out the part about the $200 referral bonus he would earn if I got the job. Little did I know that with the high turnover in the fast-food industry, I had a darn good chance of getting hired. This wasn't NASA, after all.

"Fine," I replied, shoulders slumping. I hated doing dishes.

I had a short interview the next evening and the friendly manager, Eric, welcomed me aboard as he granted me my minimum-wage job. A whole three dollars and thirty-five cents an hour. I was ecstatic. My first job plus a free meal every four hours. I could have a Big Mac or a Quarter-Pounder with Cheese, fries, and a Coke at the end of my part-time shift.

I pretended not to think about what Ammi would say if she knew I was enjoying meat that was not *halal*. I also had this growing guilt about the debt I owed Allah, because prior to getting my US visa, I promised him I was going to pray 100 *rakats* (installments) of *namaz* (prayers). However, I quit after fourteen prayers and felt I was running a tab with God. I made a mental note to try to keep up better with my prayers.

Neither Assad nor Farhan prayed five times a day. We were busy, modern Muslim students, and while we all respected our faith, one thing we had in common with most of our fellow Pakistani students at UTA was our desire to succeed in the American system first and worry about our faith later.

At McDonald's, picking up on rules, workstations, and customer-service protocols came much more easily to me than I had expected. It was hard work. I had never held a job, but I loved the pace of it and appreciated the way the managers and fellow employees spoke to me. It took time to adjust to doing menial tasks such as sweeping the floor, jobs that only the poorest of the poor performed in Pakistan. Ironically, I was now economically disadvantaged as well. My father had written to give me the news about next year's expenses.

"Dear Chippy," he wrote, addressing me by a nickname he had given me in childhood. "You are going to have to be on your own financially beginning next year. I hope you will be able to manage and maintain good grades."

A knot formed in my stomach as I read this and considered the implications. Then came the kicker.

"Please forward us your transcripts. Your mother and I enjoy showing them to the family."

I didn't fully appreciate our family's financial situation. Abboo always kept this information private. But the message was loud and clear—there was no safety net. Meanwhile, Texas international student rates had tripled since I arrived almost five months ago. This had been in the works for quite some time, but Abboo didn't know this, nor could he have done anything about it even if he did. Like most parents from far-off Asian countries sending their boys to America, my parents had an ostrich-with-its-head-in-the-sand attitude. They simply expected me to survive just as my cousins had before me. What they did not understand was that it was a very different time in America.

For instance, I heard that some fellows who had entered the US years before me had entered into "paper marriages." This is where you pay an American citizen to marry in order to achieve permanent-resident status. Green card holders had it made in America. They paid in-state tuition rates, could compete for higher-paying jobs, could buy property, and much more. However, the INS had grown wise to such strategies and the days of immigration gymnastics were long gone. Permanent residency based on marriage now required staying married a minimum of two years and concluded with an interview to confirm that the couple's union was genuine.

As I swept the floor, two of the most eligible girls from my American history class pulled into the store parking lot—in a BMW. My heart sank.

There's no way I can let them see me like this.

I had to disappear.

Quick, think fast. The restroom. I think it needs a good mopping.

I made an executive decision to spend the next thirty minutes giving the restroom floor and mirror a thorough cleaning until the girls left. Although intellectually I understood that a job was a job, I was not prepared to believe that the girls would see me as an equal once they knew I was a fast-food worker. From where I came, the servers never married their customers who were considered the elites of society.

There was, however, someone I fancied that wore the same red polyester uniform I did. Lindsey Cummings was an attractive eighteen-year-old brunette, and at five-foot-four she made me feel tall. She had a lovely smile which she used with great skill with customers, managers, and me.

"Wow, you must be smart to be studying computer science," she said, batting her long eyelashes. Somehow, she seemed more approachable than those girls in my American history class. Maybe it was the knowledge that she was not college-bound and had only completed high school.

Lindsey, her sister, Sofia, and her mother had moved to Texas from Charlotte, North Carolina. Her father, an alcoholic, had abandoned the family when the girls were young. He would appear from time to time in a drunken stupor, looking for money. I would later learn that this was an oft-repeated script in many broken American families.

Lindsey and I hit it off immediately. When she learned I was a Muslim, she told me that she too had been a religious person growing up and had gone to the First Methodist church and read the Bible. I found all this "first" business quite confusing. Churches had names like First Methodist, First Baptist, and First Presbyterian. And then there were groups like the Church of Jesus Christ of Latter-day Saints and the Jehovah's Witnesses. From a distance, they all seemed the same to me, so I immediately categorized Lindsey and her family as Christians. Ammi had warned me about the many changes and alterations that had been made to the Bible by the different Christian denominations—obvious evidence of the distortions in the Christian faith.

I paid for everything on our dates, and Lindsey was thankful and accepting of this gesture. I saw other couples doing this as well, so it seemed like the normal pattern. However, I was spending my upcoming semester's tuition. I didn't care. Lindsey was pretty and allowed me to forget my problems. With her, I again felt tall, dark, and handsome.

As my debt accumulated, I succumbed to those wonderful pieces of plastic that fit snugly in your wallet and let you buy anything you want without having to pay cash or write a check. "No credit required," said the credit card ads. "Transfer your balance today." Student credit cards were even pitched as being a wise move for establishing credit history. I was torn between Visa or MasterCard, so I got one of each. And my spending on credit began.

The best part of having credit cards was the minimum payment. I could manage twenty-five dollars each month and not worry about paying the entire bill. That flexibility was not available, however, with my phone bill. Assad was furious with me for not being able to pay my portion and I began borrowing money from Farhan.

I needed a car for dates, so I called Aslam Bhai and got a loan from him. Lindsey's uncle let me make an offer on his Mitsubishi Galant. It was a piece of junk that looked like it had a million miles on it, but it was drivable. I had no idea how to evaluate cars. In Pakistan, our chauffeur took care of such details. The car promptly broke down and my mountain of debt continued to pile up.

Lindsey suggested we buy a vehicle together and be co-signatories on it. After all, we were now going "steady," as her mom called it. They regularly invited me over for dinner. Soon we were joint owners of a brand-new sporty Pontiac Fiero, one of the worst-rated cars of the day. The debt ceiling continued to rise.

Things weren't going well on the school front, either. In Pakistan, most tests were essay tests, my preferred style. For example, a physics test had three parts. First, you wrote about Newton's second law of motion. Then you defined the elements of the equation. And finally, you solved a problem where you had most of the variables save one, and you solved for that missing variable such as speed or velocity.

My first physics test at UTA was all problems:

A man is running down the beach at two meters per second. He sees a monkey on the thirty-foot-tall palm tree. The monkey launches a coconut from the tree at a projectile angle of sixty-seven degrees and the coconut promptly hits the man on the head at a velocity of 10 meters per second. Please determine how much work is done.

What was this? Of course, it would have helped if I had attended the class session on vectors. Unfortunately, I was with Lindsey clubbing until two a.m. the night before. School nights meant nothing to her and her sister, a high school dropout. They both wanted to party after their shifts were over.

I received my first F in physics.

Panic set in as I ran into some different challenges with my Programming in Pascal course. My professor was a doctoral student, like Pitts.

Here we go again.

But instead of literature, this guy was determined to teach me American sports. He was hell-bent on teaching us bowling—not the cricket kind, mind you—but the American kind with a ball and ten pins.

The project: to write a pascal program that computes bowling frames. I'd never bowled in my life.

Are you kidding me?

I was barely squeaking out a C in the class. Meanwhile, Ammi and Abboo were demanding transcripts to showcase what their brilliant son in America was doing.

In American History I was doing slightly better, maintaining a B, which was in no small measure due to my study-group partner, Anita Sharma. Anita bordered on being a child prodigy. Of Indian descent, she graduated from high school at sixteen, at the top of her class. Her father was a cardiovascular surgeon and her mother played cello in the local symphony.

Anita was carrying the weight of the world on her shoulders. Her parents, particularly her father, expected her to continue at the same pace and graduate from UTA with a double-major in three years. Then they expected her to head off to medical school at Johns Hopkins. Her whole life was charted for her by others, another pattern I had observed in my short time in America.

Anita was miserable. She had a boyfriend, but she barely had time to see him. As we approached finals week, Anita and I were supposed to meet mid-week to prep for the upcoming final. But Anita never showed up. It was not like her to miss our session. I was concerned but assumed something must have happened. Perhaps she had taken ill. As I entered my apartment, the phone was ringing. It was Nazneen.

"Ali, I just got off the phone with the FBI. Have they called you yet?"

My heart skipped a beat. "The FBI, as in the *Federal Bureau of Investigation?*"

"Yes, they were trying to locate you and called my job. I am listed as your emergency contact. What's that about?"

"I have no idea," I stammered, my mind racing.

Visions of deportation flashed before my eyes. Life for a disgraced, middle-class Pakistani son, and an only child to boot, that is sent back home after a couple of semesters in the United States was going to be a fate worse than death.

No sooner had I hung up from chatting with Nazneen than my phone rang again. I stared at it for what felt like a hundred rings before picking up the receiver.

"Hello, is this Mr. Master?" inquired a very mature-sounding voice. The tone was neither hostile nor friendly. Just neutral.

"Yes. Yes sir. That's me."

"Mr. Master, this is Captain Henley of the UTA campus police department. Would you mind coming into our office to answer a few questions?" The tone was still very courteous, I thought.

We agreed to meet immediately, and I headed there after hanging up. The fact that they wanted me to come over gave me some odd form of comfort.

At least they don't think I am some type of flight risk.

Nevertheless, I felt waves of fear that I had not experienced since interacting with the immigration officer at JFK. Still, I was hopeful.

There's bound to be a mistake here.

A well-dressed assistant ushered me into Captain Henley's office. The shiny nameplate outside the door left no doubt that I was entering the office of an important person. Three tall men were inside having hushed conversations. One of them sat at a desk and wore the familiar campus police uniform. I assumed he was the captain. The other two were in dark suits with crisp shirts and ties.

The captain immediately stood up and shook my hand firmly. "Welcome, Mr. Master. Please have a seat," he gestured to an empty chair, evidently set there for this conversation.

I felt unusually calm, thanks to his professional demeanor.

"Mr. Master, these two gentlemen are from the FBI and they have a few questions about Anita Sharma. She has been missing since Saturday night."

I quickly calculated. *That's five days.*

The older of the two suits spoke to me.

"Mr. Master, I'm Special Agent Matthews and this is Special Agent Nichols," pointing to his partner. "Thank you for coming in. Let me first start by saying that you don't need to worry. You are not in any trouble and are not being investigated for a crime. We know you and Anita are acquaintances and classmates and we just wanted to see if you had any idea of her whereabouts."

A sea of calm washed over me as I heard him utter those words. Such professionalism. I was in awe. I wanted to help them in any way I could and said as much to them. Unfortunately, there was very little I could tell them that they didn't already know. Anita was under immense pressure. She had no time, save for studying. She hated the pressure her father put her under. She wasn't even sure she wanted to be a doctor. She liked helping young children and had spoken of being a speech therapist.

"Did she ever speak of running away to you?" Nichols inquired.

"No. Not that I can recall."

The interview lasted only ten minutes, but its dignity and the distinct feeling that I was being treated as innocent until proven guilty left a lasting impression on me. I had heard of this amazing principle found in Western jurisprudence, but to experience it was hard to express in words. This nation of laws business was proving to be as advertised.

If this were one of the notorious police stations back home and a rich girl affiliated with a poor male student had gone missing, he would be stripped, placed on a block of ice, and beaten with a rubber hose until he either confessed to the knowledge of her whereabouts, suffered enough to convince the police that he was truly innocent, or blurted out a fake confession simply to end the pain.

I never saw Captain Henley or the FBI agents again after that day, but Anita's parents did pay me a visit at two in the morning. Her father wanted to search my apartment personally. Her mother was clearly distressed but was far more subdued than he.

Not knowing my full rights, I did not object to him coming inside and looking through my entire apartment while Assad and Farhan, rudely awakened from sleep, gaped at the scene. I could tell from the father's facial expressions that he was carrying a huge burden of guilt. Much was left unsaid between him and his daughter, and I felt sad for him. He was just another example of an Asian father trying to push his offspring to greater heights, but failing to listen to his child's heart, failing to comprehend the crushing weight of those heavy expectations.

I immediately thought of Abboo. Although they were opposites in personality—this man being the strong controlling type while my father was passive and retiring—the result felt much the same. Even here, thousands of miles away, I could feel the pressure to perform, to live up to expectations, to provide a return and not squander this one-in-a-million chance to achieve the American dream.

To my immense relief, I heard through some classmates that the FBI found Anita three days later. She had suffered a nervous breakdown of sorts and persuaded her boyfriend to run away with her and hide in a remote cabin at Big Bend Park. No arrests were made.

Football season was in full swing, and I honestly couldn't figure out this sport. These huge—some even fat—human beings faced each other on the field. The man in the middle, squatting behind the fat guys, would shout out a bunch of gibberish, and everyone would run at the opposing team, resulting in a pile-up of humanity.

The crowd would go wild. Then they would set up to do it all over again.

The ball wasn't round, and they rarely kicked it, yet it was called *football*. I decided that I would try to better understand this game someday. Assad had far more understanding of it than Farhan. However, in his usual stoic style, Assad didn't have the time to explain it to me.

Along with football season came the warnings at my store about the infamous, Arlington High vs. Lamar High annual food fight. I was told that our store was the designated battleground for this annual rite-of-passage that occurred after the football game between the two schools. Not knowing what to expect, I didn't think much about it. The police officers arriving at the store prior to the postgame festivities should have been a hint.

Yellow buses, full of rambunctious high school students, arrived shortly after the game. I was in awe of how many students a single bus could carry. One group was rowdy, giddy with their victory; the other, sullen. The tension was palpable.

The students ordered hundreds of milkshakes, fries, and hamburgers, and for the first fifteen or twenty minutes, the food pretty much went where it was meant to go. Then one of the biggest guys on the Arlington side, still wearing his cleats and uniform, threw his half-full chocolate milkshake straight at a gorgeous blonde Lamar cheerleader sitting on the other side of the store.

Instantly, food was flying everywhere, and unfortunately, I had picked the most inopportune time to empty the lobby trash. The entire episode lasted less than a minute, but the mess was awe-inspiring. Food covered the floor, windows, players, cheerleaders and, of course, me.

After the students cleared out, we had to shut down the store for two hours to clean up. I wondered if we made or lost money. As I saw all the food wasted during this debacle, and thought of all the starving in my country, righteous anger brewed inside me. On the flip side, I saw players from both sides laughing out loud as they cursed each other. I had to admit, it was certainly a far healthier way to vent in contrast to how things often went at Karachi University. In Pakistan someone usually got shot when two opposing student bodies faced off.

Things between Lindsey and me were getting more complicated by the day. She was furious about the incident with Anita.

"Why is her father coming to your place? Were you sleeping with her behind my back?"

"Huh? Of course not!" I replied, offended by the accusation.

This had become a pattern. She didn't want me sitting next to girls in American History. She also thought I was attracted to Sheila, the assistant manager at our store. She didn't understand why I had to study after class, especially with others. She constantly wanted to go clubbing, even though she knew I was up to my eyeballs in debt. And she always had the car, so I couldn't go anywhere unless I rode the bicycle Aslam had given me. We fought almost daily. How could something so good fall apart so fast?

Nazneen wisely dropped the hammer like a good Pakistani sister should. "Lindsey is codependent, Ali. And it's likely got a lot to do with her alcoholic father. She never received the love and trust of a nurturing home, and she is now relying on you to provide it. You need to get out, and soon."

What? Codependent? This was heavy stuff. I was barely an adult myself. And what about me? No one had taught me that what happened to you during childhood could impact you well into adulthood. Was I the blind leading the blind?

Nazneen, like the rest of my family, including my parents, had no knowledge of my sexual abuse growing up. My childhood had hardly been a bastion of security. And I quickly pushed aside thoughts of my own dysfunctionality, just as I had those dark feelings of guilt and pain that I had experienced in Lahore many years earlier. I truly believed I was emotionally fine. I didn't know any other way.

Look at me, after all. Here I am trying to make it on my own in America. Many others couldn't have made it even this far.

I decided then that I had to act on my cousin's sage advice, but it proved to be harder than I could imagine.

Over the coming months, things got progressively worse. I was skipping classes regularly. I manufactured fake transcripts to send to my parents to hide my poor grades. I stayed out late with Lindsey all the time.

It was a vicious cycle. We would fight. We would make up. It was difficult for me to pull away from the physical side of the relationship. In Karachi, I'd had girlfriends before, but the relationships were always chaperoned. I'd never had this kind of intoxicating, destructive freedom. I realized how naïve my parents were. Trusting my two older cousins to shepherd my American existence was like trying to put out a three-alarm fire with a water pistol.

I finally decided I'd had enough, and late one Saturday night in my apartment after we'd had some tequila to drink and were in the midst of yet another argument about something mundane, such as why I didn't have the money to pay for an oil change for the car, I spit out the words, "I don't think we should see each other anymore."

Tears instantly welled in her eyes. "You what?" She looked incredulous. "It's Sheila at the store, isn't it?" she wailed. "I knew it!" Her voice was now shrill. Thankfully, Assad and Farhan were not at home.

"No, it's not. I just don't want you in my life any more, Lindsey." I found myself getting angry that she wasn't making this easy for me. This was not going well at all.

"I can't believe you are doing this to me. I *love* you, Ali. Don't you understand?" She was growing hysterical.

We went back and forth for at least forty-five minutes, and Lindsey was now crying uncontrollably. I had no idea how to transition to the can't-we-just-be-friends discussion.

How does one do that?

I never could have imagined what happened next. We were in my bedroom with Lindsey sitting on my bed about a foot away from the nightstand, where I had a lamp that was missing a lampshade. Lindsey screamed and snatched the lamp at its base. She smashed the glass of the light-bulb and looked as though she was going to stab her face with it. As if by instinct, I sprang into action and wrestled the lamp away from her. I had no idea if she was going to follow through, but I wasn't about to wait to find out.

"Stop! Stop! It's okay!" I shouted, still stunned by what had just happened. I put my arm around her and spoke softly. "It's okay. I am not going anywhere."

I sat there on the bed consoling her for what seemed like an eternity. Then we started kissing, thus ending the horrible episode, at least for her. But I felt the walls closing in on me. I was trapped, and there seemed to be no exit in sight, save one.

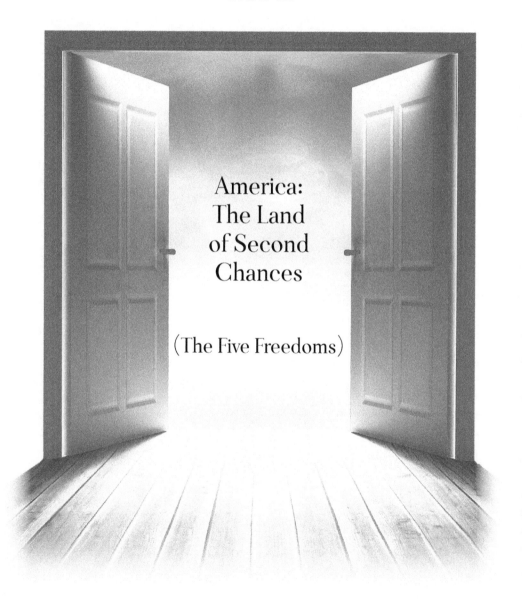

PART III

America:
The Land
of Second
Chances

(The Five Freedoms)

Chapter 5
FREEDOM TO FAIL

The image of the dead security guard still haunted me.

It happened a few years before I left for Texas. Political mayhem was reaching new heights in Karachi. Political elites often used warring factions such as the *Muttahida Quami Movement* (MQM) and the student-run *Islami Jamiat-e-Talaba* (IJT) as pawns to exact revenge on each other.[13]

One evening, as several of us had just wrapped up a street cricket game, we heard loud gunshots coming from the neighborhood just up the hill from my street. About a hundred yards out, Jamal and I crouched behind my dad's car as we saw a minivan filled with green-bandana-clad IJT students, armed with machine guns, zoom up the street, moving away from us and firing their AK-47s in the air.

In Pakistan, whether it be rioters, wedding partiers or religious zealots, everyone was obsessed with firing weapons in the air. Many a wedding had ended in tragedy with such ill-advised celebrations, but that never stopped them.

Jamal and I watched the IJT minivan disappear, and after five minutes I concluded that it would be safe to come out. The students would be long gone by now and I needed a book from the library. Jamal had to run some errands for his family and left in another direction.

The tiny storefront library was a ten-minute walk from my street, and as I arrived, I was shocked by what I saw. Not ten feet from me, lying on the dirty ground, was a dead man surrounded by a small crowd that included children. Bullet wounds riddled his chest and abdomen. He was dressed in the dark grey *shalwar-kameez* worn by local security guards. Blood was everywhere, and his

67

old shotgun lay on the ground nearby. Flies were already buzzing about his dark, mustached face. His eyes, fortunately, were closed.

I was stunned and couldn't turn away from the scene. I overheard the crowd buzzing about the fact that he was one of two victims. The primary target, a local official opposed by the IJT, was shot in the stomach three times. A group of his supporters had just rushed the councilman to the hospital in their private car. He was expected to live. His security guard was not so fortunate.

I lay in a clean bed in the Arlington Memorial Hospital emergency room reflecting on the dead security guard. I couldn't help contrasting my good fortune with his situation. It took the ambulance only seven minutes to show up to Lindsey's aunt's apartment after she frantically dialed 911. The security guard had been dead far longer than that and there wasn't a siren to be heard. He had been assaulted by AK-47s while I had been the victim of a self-initiated and poorly-executed plan to slash my own wrist using a sharp kitchen knife.

Thank God for my poor technical skills and low biology IQ. I completely missed both the radial and the ulnar arteries. The largest damage was done to my wallet—the cost of nine stitches. As I lay there alone waiting for the nurse to clear me, I was thankful for the peace and quiet. Lindsey's family had forbidden her from staying with me. I didn't want anyone around anyway, at least not anyone who knew me.

The situation had spun out of control rather quickly. My debt continued to climb, and my grades slid downward. Lindsey refused to give me any personal space or let me have any time to study. The people-pleaser in me couldn't draw boundaries or find a way out of the relationship. One break-up effort had led yet again to Lindsey threatening to hurt herself, this time by attempting to jump off my second-floor balcony. Again, I caught her in the nick of time. I didn't know if she intended to go through with such threats, but I wasn't about to carry the guilt of finding out by not intervening.

Three calamities ultimately landed me in Arlington Memorial. First, I slept through my physics final. The exam started at 8:30 a.m., but I woke up at noon after fighting with Lindsey until three. I rushed to Dr. Martin's office to make excuses and beg for him to let me take an "Incomplete" in the class, but he would have none of it. Mr. Pitt's prophetic words, "You will never succeed in the American collegiate system," resonated in my brain at that moment. Strike one.

Not knowing how I was going to face my parents with this disgraceful news weighed heavily on me. I was not equipped to deal with such adversity and conflict, so I retreated into a dark shell and ignored my work schedule. I missed one day, then another, and finally another, all without finding the emotional strength to inform my employer. I was a "no call, no show" for three straight days, a terminable offense. To make matters worse, Assad let the phone bill lapse to teach me a lesson and the phone service was cut off. I had no way to call the restaurant or Nazneen. I finally begged one of the neighbors to let me call the store only to learn that I had been fired. Strike two.

But it was the news Lindsey gave me that shook me the most when I tried, once again, to beg her to leave me alone.

"I think I may be pregnant," she blurted, eyeing me carefully for my reaction. I sat there, stunned by this revelation.

"Are—are you sure?" I asked, my voice rising. I felt angry, as if being pregnant were her fault, not to mention a deliberate attempt to sabotage my life. My mind raced through the implications and options.

"I'm late by a few days," she said in a casual tone that irritated the hell out of me. *Does she not have a clue how this would destroy me?*

The "Land of Opportunity" had quickly become the land of consequences. Every action or inaction had a consequence in this country.

Breaking the news to my parents about failing physics started to sound like a cakewalk in comparison.

I resisted the urge to ask, "Are you sure it's mine?"

How could it not be? She never leaves me alone.

I was no Michael Douglas, but I felt that I was living my own version of the movie *Fatal Attraction*.[14]

We were at her aunt's place to babysit her two young children. Thankfully, both were napping. I was getting angrier by the minute.

Surely this is a ploy to prevent me from breaking up with her.

I felt like I was watching my entire life circling the drain. It had been barely a year since I landed on American soil, yet in so many ways, I felt I had aged a decade. The "Land of Opportunity" had quickly become the land of consequences. Every action or inaction had a consequence in this country. If you don't pay your bill, your phone line is disconnected. If you don't drop a course in time, you receive an F. If you don't call in to work, you're fired. If you don't set physical boundaries with your girlfriend, you become a father. I could barely raise myself, let alone someone else.

I couldn't take it anymore. This was not the life I'd dreamed of. Nor was this the American college experience I expected. At some point during our fourth or fifth argument that night, I snapped. I wanted the pain and conflict to end, and I most definitely wanted Lindsey to feel guilty for wrecking my life. I had seen a set of knives in the kitchen. I pushed Lindsey back with my right hand and opened the knife drawer as Lindsey screamed, begging me to stop. Seconds later, I was bleeding profusely from my left wrist. Dizziness overcame me, and I fell.

Before I lost consciousness, I overheard Lindsey trying to explain to the 911 operator that there had been an accident. She was crying, which felt good. The next thing I knew, paramedics were taping my wrist shut and asking me whether I wanted to pay the hundred and fifty dollars to ride in the ambulance or if I could make my way to the hospital on my own.

"He's going to be okay," I heard one of them saying.

As tempting as it was to take my first ride in an ambulance, I decided to pass and have Lindsey's neighbor take me. Lindsey, thankfully, had to stay with the kids. She was, for the moment, a changed person and was being incredibly sweet to me.

Hey, I should do this more often.

I discarded any ideas of repeating the incident after the woman at the checkout desk informed me that the bill would total nearly seven hundred fifty dollars. I wrote a check knowing that there was at least a fifty-fifty chance of it bouncing higher than a cricket bouncer (a fast ball bowled to intimidate the batsman). Nevertheless, I walked out feeling an odd sense of optimism, like something new and good was about to begin.

Something new did begin. Or I should say, something old did not begin. Lindsey kept her distance, mostly due to her family's insistence, but also because she knew it was over. Still, it took me repeatedly begging my roommates to take her clubbing before she finally acknowledged she had met somebody else.

"His name is Tony," she said in a chirpy voice. Then, she added a jab. "He loves to dance."

I wasn't the best of dancers.

Mission accomplished. God bless Tony.

"You know I will always love you, don't you?" she added.

I nodded but said nothing. I had never uttered those three words to her. Nor did I intend to now.

She kept the Pontiac Fiero since she still had a job. I walked away with the television and the VCR we had purchased together. Thus ended the sad saga of Lindsey Cummings.

As it turned out, Lindsey wasn't pregnant after all. As I share my American journey and look back at the many twists and turns it took, this was one disaster from which the hand of Providence chose to spare me and for which I am eternally grateful. Three decades later, I believe with every fiber of my being that life begins at conception. Back then, I was a nominal Muslim. In Islam I was taught that the soul enters the human body after four months of gestation and that abortion becomes *haram* (forbidden) only after that point.[15]

> *One of America's greatest gifts to me and to millions of others is the ability to choose, to make decisions about a wide range of things: where we live, what we study, or what occupation we pursue.*

That fateful night before I landed at Arlington Memorial, I argued with Lindsey about our options. Her inclination was to keep the baby if she was pregnant. Although I was unsure, I leaned the other way. I do not know ultimately where I would have landed. I was barely twenty and in self-preservation mode. I doubt I had my birth mother's strength of character. She chose to carry me for nine difficult months despite having polio. According to Islamic law one can abort a fetus even after the four-month period if the baby is predicted to have a deformity.[16] Many doctors predicted that for me. But Alina, my mother, was resolute in her determination to bear me, even at the risk of death.

One of America's greatest gifts to me and to millions of others is the ability to choose, to make decisions about a wide range of things: where we live, what we study, or what occupation we pursue. Sometimes though, as in my case, the best gift may be to be spared from having to make any choice at all.

I was terribly homesick, and my parents knew it. They scrounged enough savings together to send me a ticket to come home to Karachi to visit. That summer, I went home for two months.

Returning to my homeland after having spent an extended amount of time in the United States was a complicated experience. People treated me differently and, in some ways, like royalty. My aunts wanted to show me off at every wedding gathering to inquisitive mothers with daughters. My uncles wanted to talk geopolitics and slam the United States for interfering in the sovereign affairs of just about every Muslim nation on the planet. Every ailment in Pakistani society was the CIA's fault. Readjusting to the heat, the filth on the streets, the disorganization, and the corruption, was miserable. I loved being back to see my friends and family, but I had a keen sense that I did not belong there any longer. Home was no longer in Karachi; it was in Arlington.

There was no way I could share my struggles with Ammi and Abboo. Their only son, their *raja*, had returned victorious for the summer after slaying the dragons of Texas.

"What's that mark on your wrist, *Beta* (son)?"

I lied, surprising even myself at the ease with which it flew out of my lips. "Oh, nothing Ammi, just an accident. I slipped and cut it on some glass. No big deal,"

"*Bohat badmash ho tum* (you are a troublemaker)," she said teasingly, and dropped the issue.

Abboo never even asked. He was more interested in hearing about my plans for graduate school, even though I was only a sophomore. Always the carrot dangling out ahead. The pressure was back, even during a summer break.

During my trip, I reconnected with some of my friends from the neighborhood and observed how their lives had changed. Jamal was working with his uncle in real estate. Salman had become a heroin addict. Faisal, an atheist. And, Sohail, the country club socialite, had grown a full beard and was teaching in a *madrasa*

(Islamic school). He was the most uncomfortable to interact with because he kept referring to America as "The Great Satan."

I got the sense that things were rapidly changing in my home country. The more innocent and carefree era I knew was being replaced by one much darker. General Zia-ul-Haq, the president of Pakistan, was an avid supporter of the Islamization of the nation.[17] I read about and saw many more religious schools. After learning about the merits of the separation of church and state in my political science class, this co-mingling of a military-leader-turned-president with religion did not sound like a good plan to me. I couldn't wait to get back to my new home in Texas. Even though I knew huge challenges awaited me there, somehow, it felt far more appealing than what I sensed was coming to Pakistan.

Upon my return to Texas, I was determined not to let the mistakes of my past define my future. Using some of my father's hard-earned cash, I transferred to a local community college in Las Colinas, a beautiful town twenty-five minutes northeast of Arlington. I loved the cozy feel of North Lake College. It was far smaller, classes were more intimate, and professors were warm and friendly.

And all this for half the cost of UTA. I guess that's why they call it community college.

I was pleasantly surprised to find that only my credit hours transferred from the university, not the failing GPA. I desperately needed a fresh start. But much to my disappointment, the smallness of the community college did not change the basic formula for college success, starting with attending classes. All of them. Then there was the turning in of assignments. On time. All of them. Then came the studying before tests. Yes, all of them. And lastly, there was taking the exams when they were scheduled.

I discovered this formula worked well for a sure B in any college course thrown at me. And with a little bit of extra credit and effort, one could even make an A. Knowing this intellectually was one thing; the execution was another. Even without Lindsey Cummings holding me back, I still struggled in my classes. My grades were starting to spiral once more, and I was utterly dejected.

In the midst of this, I discovered the freedom of changing majors. I went from Computer Science to Chemistry to Management Information Systems to Creative Writing and then to Business in an alarmingly short period of time.

I appreciated this academic freedom to experiment. It fascinated me that a person could make a living in America by doing so many things. In Pakistan, I'd been forced into pre-engineering at the age of twelve. Even though I didn't enjoy technical math or biology, that was the only option presented to me. It was refreshing to try so many classes, but I would only try them for a short while and then despise the homework, the reading, and the assignments. There it was again, that high-pitched, piercing voice of Mr. Pitts from UTA telling me that I would never make it. I was beginning to believe him, and my grades were confirming his opinion.

It was as if the discipline switch in me was flipped off. I needed a reboot badly, but I simply didn't know how. It was a skill I had never acquired.

Months flashed by. During my second semester at North Lake, instead of attending more classes, I was drawn to participation in student government. The college had a sizeable population of multinationals. Countries like Iran, India, China, Liberia, Laos, Ghana, and Pakistan were all represented. I found myself actively engaging with these students. They knew nothing of my academic struggles. I came up with ideas for activities, fundraisers, and social events. The students all seemed willing to follow my lead and enjoyed being around me. I felt affirmed and encouraged.

One of the deans suggested to me that the students should form an International Student Union (ISU) with bylaws, officers, and such. Someone encouraged me to run for president, and I found this idea enticing. Carl, a student from Liberia, was also interested in the office. An election date was set, giving us three weeks to convince our fellow students to vote for us. I enjoyed persuading students and lobbying for my vision for the ISU. I won the election by a good margin and asked Carl to be my vice-president. It was my very first experience with leadership, and I loved it. It was also the first challenge I had been successful at in a long time.

Being popular on campus and well-known to the professors and administration started to propel me to unnatural behavior: attending classes.

"I didn't know you were in my physics class," said Martha, a gorgeous gal from Ghana. "Let's do study group together."

"Uhm…I am not sure I can make it," was my immediate excuse. My relationship fears were still overpowering.

Martha wasn't about to give up this quickly and brought in support. "Oh, come on. Sonia and Diana are part of the group, too." Sonia and Diana were part of my student council.

I succumbed.

As it turned out, the three of them had an average GPA of 3.75. I didn't realize you could be good-looking *and* make good grades. Lindsey had always presented that as a binary choice. I learned that most of them spent hours each day studying. They also had part-time jobs and managed to be active in either student activities or athletics.

Later that week, I received a phone call from the student counselor assigned to me, asking to meet. Sarah knew me and had attended several of our ISU events. "You are obviously very bright, Ali, so what's going on with your grades?"

I didn't have a good answer.

She recommended that I attend Dr. Bradley's remedial class that started in a few weeks. "In fact, I have already enrolled you," she said with a kind smile that said, *I am not taking no for an answer.* And there it was, a gentle kick in the pants from someone who believed in me.

Dr. William Bradley was a remarkable man: about sixty, full of energy and enthusiasm, with several PhDs to his name. He had also worked for the FBI and traversed the world in a Cessna plane that he piloted. Dr. Bradley, or Bill as he insisted on being called, took an immediate interest in me. He didn't ask me why or how I found myself in a remedial class in a junior college. The goal was to help me learn the basic skills of time management, writing, reading, communication, and presentation.

The class was only a single-credit hour, but for me it was a life-saver. Perhaps it was Bill taking a personal interest in me like no one ever had. Perhaps it was this man's achievements and character that made me want to impress him. Perhaps it was that first A on the first test, circled in red-ink with a smiley face on it and the words, "Well done."

I aced the class. It was to be the first of my many As at North Lake and beyond. Sometimes, all it takes is for someone to believe in you.

The confidence I gained through my academic and student-leadership success at North Lake sent me seeking a job in South Arlington. I found myself, once again, drawn to the golden arches. Because of my previous termination, I didn't expect to be hired, but McDonald's is a busy place. When I explained my situation, with my new-found confidence, the store manager agreed to offer me the job, and a much-needed second chance.

This time around, I poured myself into the job. I found the similarity between working at one McDonald's versus the other fascinating. The cooking procedures, equipment, cash registers, menu and store language were identical. In Pakistan in the 1980s, there was no such thing as a franchise model. Every restaurant was unique. But I found franchise consistency to be a distinct advantage, as I quickly mastered all the workstations.

I loved collecting all the pins awarded for mastering the different workstations: counter, grill, drive-thru, and more. What intrigued me even more was the clear promotion path before me. I could move from crew-person, to trainer, to swing (shift) manager, to assistant manager, to general manager.

Then there was our city manager, Pat, a tall blonde in her mid-forties. She oversaw all eight corporate stores and was a no-nonsense general. She had started as crew person serving at the counter a mere nine years before. She had decided to return to the workforce after her kids were grown. Coming from a male-dominated society, I had never seen a female leader in action, and it was impressive. Above her in rank, there was the big boss, Joe. He ran three states and forty-seven stores. And where did Joe start eighteen years ago? As a crew-person. Even Fred Turner, the CEO of McDonald's, started on the grill.[18]

I found those facts extremely motivating. They gave me a vision for a path forward. In Pakistan, a person working the grill in a fast-food restaurant would never dream of becoming a manager, let alone the chief executive of the enterprise.

What a remarkable system.

Inscribed on a plaque on the wall of the store were these inspiring words from the founder, Ray Kroc:

Nothing in the world can take the place of Persistence. Talent will not; nothing is more common than unsuccessful men with talent. Genius will not; unrewarded genius is almost a proverb. Education will not; the world is full of educated derelicts. Persistence and Determination alone are omnipotent.[19]

I found these words to be both propelling and reassuring. What resonated most with me, though, were the real-life examples of folks around me rising from their circumstances to better themselves.

Six months later, my big day arrived. I was a swing-manager-in-training. It was Saturday lunch hour. My heart raced as the lobby buzzed with customers. Pat was on the schedule to pay a surprise visit to "shop" my shift. I moved quickly through the store, running through my mental checklist. Parking lot clean? Check. Lobby clean? Check. What percentage is labor running? (We always had to stay below a percentage of sales). I needed to send Joey, who was working the counter, on his break. Then Pat walked in slowly, like the grim reaper. Her face showed me nothing. For my part, I kept calm and continued to serve the customers. She then called me up for my quiz.

"What's the price of a garden salad?" she asked. I wasn't expecting that one.

"Uhm…three dollars and thirty-five cents?" I guessed nervously.

Crap. I'm dead.

"What's the temperature on the Filet-O-Fish? she continued.

That one I knew. "Four hundred and thirty-five degrees." I said with a confident smile.

In the middle of her inquisition, Pat was distracted by and began visiting with a customer whom she knew from her prior life. I stood there awaiting my fate for three whole minutes that felt like an eternity.

Finally, she turned back to me and said, "You can take that 'trainee' off your name tag now," showing a rare smile, but only for a brief second.

Just then Chris, one of the assistant managers, announced to the entire store over the PA system that I had been promoted. The entire team and even some customers cheered.

And that's how I became a swing manager. Persistence and determination. There was still some of that left in my tank. It was a happy day.

With the raise I received from my promotion, I was able to start paying my bills on time. Assad showed me how to repair my credit by getting a credit card that I would pay off every month. Friends with more experience encouraged me to call some of my creditors, such as the telephone company, and ask them to forgive the debt. Although skeptical, I made the call. Amazingly, they waived a large amount. I didn't even know that was possible. Back home, I would very likely have been beaten up if I couldn't pay my bills. *Grace* is not a word often used in the Urdu vocabulary.

Although I never had to file for bankruptcy, I did learn about it in my finance class. Again, I was astounded by the instruments of forgiveness and second chances found in the American economic system.

As I studied in my American History class, the notion of forgiveness, redemption, and of allowing men to try again was not unique to business or finance. It was a road well-traveled by many. One of the most remarkable examples of this virtue was found in none other than the sixteenth president of the United States, Abraham Lincoln. I couldn't believe my eyes when I saw his timeline. Between 1832 and 1860, Lincoln ran for public office a total of eleven times. During this twenty-eight-year span, he lost an astounding eight times, including the time just before being elected president.[20] That spoke volumes to me, not only about the perseverance of the man, but about the culture and the people. Like no other nation, America allowed for failure on the road to success.

I learned many inspiring stories of great Americans who experienced enormous failure prior to achieving success. Thomas Edison was fired from several jobs on his way to failing one thousand times before inventing the lightbulb. Henry Ford went broke five times prior to reaching success in the car industry. Even Ray Kroc was a failure as a salesman prior to discovering McDonald's. Stories of persistence and determination from the past, but more importantly from the present, were everywhere.

Even American college sports had "walk-on" players. Any athletes that felt they had the talent and the confidence to compete for a slot on a team could try out, even with little to no prior experience. The fact that college athletics offered the option to walk-on said a lot to me. In Pakistan, for opportunity to come your way, it wasn't a matter of talent or skill alone but was more about who you knew and whether you spoke the right dialect or hailed from the right province.

Over my three decades of living in America, this pattern of men and women experiencing colossal failure, yet rising from the ashes to experience unparalleled success still lives on. While their secret to success is almost always the ability to persevere, the American willingness to offer a second chance, and the redemptive freedom found in her systems, be it politics, business, academics, entertainment, or sports, serves as a powerful and unique catalyst for success. This desire, even eagerness, of Americans to root for the underdog is singularly special and demands further examination.

In America, it was possible to find success after failure and, although achieving success was not easy, everyone had the opportunity to seek it.

Back in the late '80s, as a struggling young immigrant in the United States, I began to understand that few things worth having come easily in America. Those who were successful, whether in academia, government, business, or television, paid a price for their success through hard work and perseverance.

For the first time, I saw a way out of my troubles. I had hope and a future. In America, it was possible to find success after failure and, although achieving success was not easy, everyone had the opportunity to seek it. This was not like back home, where the transition from blue to white collar was a virtual impossibility. There, the chasm between the haves and the have-nots can last for generations.

America, on the other hand, offered that rare and precious freedom to fail and start over.

Chapter 6

FREEDOM TO LOVE

It was a warm Texas morning on Wednesday, August 17, 1988. Two years had passed since I set foot in the United States. So much had transpired in such a short time, but in terms of sheer experience it felt like two *long* years.

That morning, I was rushing to get ready to go to the store because I had no classes on Wednesdays. That was one of the many things I loved about McDonald's. They looked at my college schedule each semester and planned shifts around it. Even as a shift-manager, I could continue my education and make a living. Workplace flexibility is yet another American freedom that many take for granted.

As I dressed, I saw the light flashing on my answering machine showing two messages. I pressed play. It was Josephine, or Josie as she liked to be called.

"Hi sweetie," she crooned in her throaty voice. "It's me…Josie. It's around eleven. Just wondering if you're gonna show up to Samantha's party tonight? See you soon." *Beep.*

I hit delete and hit play again for the second message, simultaneously trying to put on my shoes. It was her again.

"Hey, it's almost midnight. I didn't think you were closing tonight. Okay. Call me tomorrow. Maybe we can catch a movie. Byeeeee." *Beep.*

I smiled and thought it was cute how she extended her "byes."

Josie and I had met at the store. She was not my official girlfriend, but she was getting close. I had been seeing several girls at the same time thanks to a vindictive rumor started by Jake, one of the other shift-managers.

Jake wanted the assistant manager job badly and saw me as his sole competition. After my experience with Lindsey, I wanted nothing to do with girls, and opted instead to hang out with my new roommate, Rahim. He was from Pakistan and was also in between girlfriends. We did everything together, and it was a relief to not have the pressure of anyone's expectations. Then Jake decided to stir things up.

"You know Ali's a fag," I overheard Jake say to one of the trainers. "He and Rahim have it going on, those two Paki faggots."

I was incensed, both at the racial slur and being labeled a homosexual when I wasn't. In the eighties in Pakistan, being labeled as gay was often literally a kiss of death. Islam prohibits homosexuality.[21]

Dark memories of men in Lahore viewing me as prey flooded back like a tsunami. I was surprised by the anger I felt. I decided then and there to prove Jake wrong. I started dating as many women as possible, and in a very overt way. Josie was exhibit A in that process.

I flipped on the TV to catch the news before heading out and immediately a photo of General Zia-ul-Haq caught my attention. The former military leader and the president of Pakistan was dead, killed in an airplane crash. I couldn't believe what the news reporter was saying: "General Zia's plane exploded ten minutes into its flight over Bahawalpur, Pakistan. US Ambassador, Arnold Raphel, was also on board along with twenty-eight others. There were no survivors."[22]

My first thought was that this was no accident. To this day, no one knows what happened. It remains one of the biggest mysteries in Pakistani politics.

I went to work in a daze after learning the news. "Will things ever change in my nation?" I wondered out loud. Nevertheless, I soon forgot about General Zia as I wrestled with life, work, dating, student union leadership, and enjoying my new raise of fifty cents an hour. That translated into a thousand dollars more per year in discretionary income. I was approaching $5.50 an hour. Chris, the assistant manager, was making over $9.00 an hour and that was my dream.

Someday that will be me.

Chris had a steady girlfriend and was about to graduate from U.T. Arlington with a business degree. He drove a new Camaro and could afford not only his monthly payments but also the oil change required every five thousand miles. He was my role model. He worked hard and played hard. That's what I viewed as the goal now. It seemed so much more stable than the off-the-rails life I lived during my freshman year. Still, something seemed empty about it all. I just couldn't put my finger on what.

New Year's was fast approaching, and the weather had turned cold in Arlington. Rahim and I were looking forward to partying hard come December 31. Any rumors that he and I were gay had been long-since put to rest. Jake had been made to look like a complete fool when his girlfriend broke up with him and started going out with Rahim.

I was elated about my new car, a pre-owned Mazda 626 with a sunroof. It was metallic blue and was the nicest-smelling car I had ever owned. I bought it from an Iranian car mechanic, Naveed, who refurbished cars from the junkyard and would then sell them to international students.

"It's the best deal I got for you, Ali," I recall him saying. "Only for you I sell for fifteen hundred dollars."

He was a Shia Muslim like me. I trusted him and agreed to a payment plan. Two weeks later the car developed an oil leak around the head, and smoke would regularly pour out from under the hood.

"The seal. You need to replace it," Aslam advised me.

"Seal?" I asked, a bit daunted. Having grown up with a chauffeur in Karachi, I was proud that I could now change the oil myself. But I knew nothing about seals.

"Yes, you need to go to an auto supply store and give them the make and model of your car," Aslam counseled over the phone. "It's not that hard. Don't drive until it's done."

Off I went to the nearest auto-parts store to pick up a seal. That was another thing that impressed me about America; you could do things yourself. In Pakistan, if I did this, I would feel responsible for starving all the poor auto-laborers who would replace a seal for five dollars.

I installed the seal on New Year's Eve but was not supposed to drive the car for eight hours while it set. However, I had a party to attend.

Surely, four hours is enough.

I drove to Fort Worth, about thirty minutes away, and saw smoke coming out from under the hood as I arrived at the party.

I'll bet it's just oil residue that Aslam Bhai told me about.

Sally—potential girlfriend candidate number two—saw me from the apartment balcony and waved for me to come up. An hour or so after we rang in 1989, I heard sirens and saw blue-and-red flashing lights in the parking lot.

"Hide the beer! Hide the beer!" screamed the mostly-underage crowd.

Somehow, I had a premonition that this wasn't about a bunch of young college students celebrating New Year's with adult beverages. I rushed down three flights of stairs and almost ran headlong into the fire chief.

"Officer, it's only an oil leak." I exclaimed, assuming one of the neighbors had called in my smoking car.

"Son, is that your blue Mazda parked up front?" the mustached chief inquired in a serious tone that made me uncomfortable.

"Uhm…yes sir," I stammered.

"Well son, I think you'd best come down with me then."

I followed the chief, and to my shock, I saw two other firemen hosing down the front of my smoking car. Water was everywhere, and the front of the car was no longer blue. Several neighbors circled my car, shaking their heads.

I recalled the warning on the instructions: "LET SEAL SET FOR A MINIMUM OF EIGHT HOURS."

The land of consequences had struck again.

Now in need of transportation, I worked out a payment plan with my former roommate's boss for his red Honda 250 dual-purpose motorbike. Never mind that I didn't have a motorcycle license. Ammi would have killed me with her bare hands if she knew I was going to be riding this bike on American highways, especially since my birth father died in a motorbike accident. But desperate times called for desperate measures. I couldn't afford another car and the bike was fuel-efficient. It was the fastest way to hit the reset button once more. I was determined not to miss school and, besides, I loved riding it. It reminded me of the good old days in Karachi when Jamal and I would rent bikes and ride. It also seemed like a nod of respect to Uncle Imran, who taught me how to ride.

To pay for the burnt Mazda and the bike, I took a second job at Wendy's. My resume as a shift manager at McDonald's made me a natural there. So, I was now juggling two jobs and school, often working the closing shift at one restaurant and getting up a few hours later to open the other store. Meanwhile, I still partied when I wasn't at work. The relationships felt hollow yet enjoyable, and that's what everyone else around me was doing—school, work, and partying.

One day as I was leaving Wendy's, I saw a police car in the parking lot next to our store. My heart beat a tick faster, remembering that I didn't have a motorbike license. But I had to get to the other store quickly, so I proceeded. Seconds after I turned onto the main street, blue lights flashed behind me.

The officer gave me six tickets: showing a white light, no license, no insurance, no inspection sticker, no helmet, and no turn signal. I begged and pleaded, citing my poverty, but to no avail. The cost of the tickets was almost the same as what I was paying for the bike. I decided to pay the tickets instead of the bike payments—it was better to walk than to be in jail—and Assad repossessed the bike on behalf of his employer.

I was getting sick of living in the land of consequences.

Rahim and Josie drove me around for many weeks while I regrouped. Eventually, I made the catch-up payments, plus interest, and was back on my Honda once more.

Not all the cops of Arlington had it in for me. It was finals week and I was still working both jobs, routinely closing one restaurant, sleeping three hours, opening the other store, and then rushing to college.

Rahim had loaned me his Nissan since it was too cold that night for riding a bike. I was returning from closing at two in the morning. I don't think I had slept much more than four hours in the previous forty-eight. The car was warm, and I dozed off at a stoplight with my foot on the brake.

The next thing I knew, I heard a knock on my window. Two police officers were waving their flashlights and urging me to step outside the vehicle.

Oh my God. Not again.

I slowly put the car in park and stepped out. Thoughts of my deportation flashed before my eyes.

I wonder if I can run a Wendy's in Karachi?

"Officers, I promise I am not drunk. Just asleep!" I wailed, as I produced my driver's license and registration for the car, which, mercifully, Rahim kept in the glove compartment.

"Walk in a straight line for us, please," the taller of the two officers said in a professional but curt tone.

I obliged, maintaining my balance.

"What street is this?" he asked.

I answered correctly.

"Can you recite the ABC's backwards?" said the other.

Fear surged through my veins.

Are you kidding me? Who can do that?

I read the officer's last name from his name tag. "Uhm, Officer Stevens, I wasn't born here. Can you please ask me another question?" I pleaded.

"How will you get to your home from here?" queried the other officer.

That one I could manage.

"Wait in the car," said Officer Stevens.

Then they both went back to their squad car with its radio crackling. Minutes passed by that felt like an eternity. I played out a range of deportation worst-case scenarios in my head.

The bacon bits on the baked potato would definitely have to go if I start a Wendy's in Karachi.

Bacon is forbidden in Islam.

"You need to get some sleep, son," Officer Stevens said as he handed back my license. He put his hand gently on my shoulder. "Get some rest and be careful, please."

"Yes sir, officer," I said, feeling an overwhelming sense of relief wash over me. I was grateful for the way the officers had treated me.

I drove home, careful to stay five miles below the speed limit all the way, while pinching my cheeks to keep myself awake. After I got home, I fell onto my bed and slept for thirteen hours straight.

The next day, I glanced at Rahim's newspaper. Rahim, who was fond of stocks, had the business section open to the stock market page. I smiled a weary smile. My life looked very much like the Dow Jones Industrial Average chart. I was up, then down, then up for a bit, then dipping down again. However, if you tracked it over time, my line had a gradual upward trajectory. Meeting Judy Fox, however, gave a completely new meaning to the word *trajectory* in my young life.

Most of us think of progress in life as forward momentum and not about turns, but a turn was precisely what was coming. I met Judy at the same blessed institution that had taught me so much—McDonald's. Her parents lived in South Arlington, a short distance from the store where I worked. Judy was a sophomore at the University of North Texas (UNT) in Denton, about an hour's drive northwest. She was home for the summer and had taken a full-time job at the store to earn extra spending money for school. Judy was a straight-A student with glowing references, no visible tattoos or body piercings, and a radiant smile. She answered every question promptly with a "Yes sir," or "Yes ma'am," during the interview.

Sometime later, while we were counting cash, Chris the assistant manager said, "So have you had Judy Fox on your shift yet?"

"No, not yet. But I think she is on this weekend," I replied. "Why?" I asked with a forced casualness, even though my curiosity was piqued.

"I think you will like her. She's...different," Chris said, grinning a knowing smile.

I scowled and gave him a friendly "back-off" look as I left for a class.

Indeed, Judy was different than any other girl I had met at the store, at school, and certainly back home in Karachi. At five-foot-six, with hazel eyes, brown hair, and a nice figure and face, she was dating material in my book. But it was her vivacious personality that held my attention. She went out of her way to delight customers and assist other team members. When her shift was over, and while she waited for a ride, she would often grab a washcloth and start cleaning off dirty tables. There was a joy about her that I found baffling.

What kinds of vitamins is she taking? I wondered.

As for Judy, I later discovered she thought I might be a rapist.

"Whaat?" I said in disbelief when months later she finally told me about her original suspicions.

Her suitemate had been assaulted by a guy from "over there" who was a manager at a McDonald's in Denton. Rather than go to jail he chose to disappear, and Judy had heard the rumor that he was working at another McDonald's somewhere.

"I was paralyzed when you first started paying attention to me, thinking you might be him," she said, chuckling. "But then I got to know you and realized it couldn't possibly be you."

I asked Judy out repeatedly, and she repeatedly rebuffed me with a polite and breezy, "No." She could spot a train wreck from a mile away.

But I was persistent. Finally, after I asked for the umpteenth time, she said, perhaps hoping to deter me, "Well, if you'd like to go to church on Sunday with my family and me, you'd be more than welcome."

I agreed immediately.

How bad can it be? Ammi taught me all I need to know about Christianity. I can totally handle this.

The visit to church was far less threatening than I expected. Judy also introduced me to her parents, John and Jean, two salt-of-the-earth Midwesterners from

Illinois. Every other kid I knew had divorced parents, but John and Jean's home oozed stability. John was an electrical engineer with an MBA. Jean was a Purdue graduate, but had been a homemaker for most of their married life.

Judy Fox   John and Jean Fox

Judy and I spent much of our time outside the store comparing notes on what I'd been taught growing up and what she had. We would visit Caelum Moor—Arlington's answer to Stonehenge—or go for ice-cream, a joy ride on my Honda, or simply visit in her beautiful backyard by a creek.

After several years in the US, I had developed a reliable radar for detecting any racist undertones. With Judy's family, I caught no hint of racism. They seemed genuinely happy to see me and regularly invited me over for dinner.

I found Judy both intellectually stimulating and daunting, particularly when it came to her unlimited arsenal of strong opinions. It seemed the girl had a point of view about everything.

"So, why did you change your major at UNT from fashion design to art education?" I asked one day as we walked around her neighborhood.

"I didn't want to spend my life helping people focus on how they look. There's so much more to people than what they wear," she replied without a second thought.

It was like that all the time. Judy had views about small things like fashion, pets, cars, paint colors, and movies. She had views about big things such as career, kids, and issues of faith. I found this all amazing and intriguing. I had never met anyone as well-grounded as she was.

On almost any topic, she would often turn and ask me, "So, what do you think about that?"

I would just smile, shrug my shoulders, and say, "I don't know. I've never thought about it before."

I was more focused on when I would get to kiss her for the first time.

I made my move a few weeks later when she came to visit her family during a three-day weekend. We had gone to a movie. As we returned to the house, it happened naturally. I opened her car door, our eyes met, and then our lips met for a moment. I didn't want to push it. Mr. Fox was home and, as non-threatening as he was, I had heard horror stories of fathers carrying shotguns to protect their daughters. We were in Texas, after all. Still, I couldn't help but feel something special was happening.

I loved how Judy would send me home to study for my accounting exam and that she, too, was focused on excelling in school. I loved the feeling of wanting to make her proud. I had never experienced a relationship that was not dependent on drinking, watching inappropriate movies, using foul language, sex, attending parties, and the like.

One day, Judy threw out the idea of going to a concert. "It's Petra, a Christian rock band, and then there's a speaker."

I had never been to a Christian concert before and had no idea what to expect. "Absolutely," I said, thinking she could give me any kind of haircut she wanted, and I would agree.

The Petra concert was at an arena downtown. It was fascinating to see a rock band singing songs about God with drums, electric guitars, and more. Growing up as a Pakistani Muslim, that was unthinkable. As it turned out, Petra was the opener for a speaker named Dr. Bill Bright of Campus Crusade for Christ. His topic for the evening was, "Why Wait?"

"What's this all about?" I whispered into Judy's ear.

"We'll find out," she said, clearly surprised by the topic.

I listened intently during the message, glancing in disbelief at Judy several times. She made no eye-contact. Instead, she was blushing a range of shades of pink.

Dr. Bright said that God created a man and a woman to become "one flesh" in the context of marriage, but not before.

Panic rushed through my brain.

Oh my God! She is a virgin! I thought those only existed back home!

After my amazement, I felt a range of emotions. First, disappointment in myself. It was too late for me. Then hope, as Judy knew of my shenanigans at the store, and yet was still willing to go out with me. Or was she? Were we actually "going out" in her mind? Then, anger. We had kissed.

I don't know about you, young lady, but where I come from, when two people kiss, it means something. It means…you and me, we've got something here.

On the drive back, Judy was apologetic.

"I had no idea that was going to be the topic. I'm so sorry."

I nodded seriously. "So…do you really believe all of that?" I asked, already knowing the answer.

"Yes," she said quietly.

"*All* of it?" I asked with friendly sarcasm and a bit of real shock.

She nodded.

"So, I'm not getting lucky with you, huh?" I asked, as we pulled up to her house. At least now I knew where we stood on that topic.

"You've got that right, buster." And she burst out laughing.

Valentine's Day

I have myself delivered as
a Christmas gift to Judy

For the next month, although sex was out of the question, we certainly enjoyed kissing. Our favorite rendezvous point was the McDonald's walk-in refrigerator.

"Meet me in the walk-in in five, over," I would say through the drive-through headset when only the two of us could hear.

"10-4," she would respond.

We'd walk out a few minutes later carrying milkshake mix or hamburger patties with grins on our faces. Judy and I had become close, too close for comfort for some who cared about her.

I used to sneak Judy away in the wee hours of the morning to go riding around Arlington on my bike after closing the store. I'd ride to the street where the Fox family lived, turn off my lights and engine, and cruise in neutral up to their house. On the nights when she was in town, I would sneak across the lawn and up to her window. The side window would open, and the window screen would pop out of its place followed by Judy, clad in her PJs. I almost felt horns growing out of my head when we would ride out. We'd ride for hours and then she would climb back through her window.

It was the end of another semester, and I wasn't sure when Judy would be back for the summer break from UNT. Her car was parked in the driveway, so it looked like I was in luck as I cruised up to the house just past midnight. I quietly approached the window, knocked, and called quietly to Judy, not realizing that she had not come home yet.

To my complete horror, instead of Judy, I heard the voice of her mother, Jean. "Ali, Judy is not here. Please go home and go to bed."

This was the first time I had heard Jean sound angry. The speed with which I made my exit would have made motocross fans proud.

Later, Judy told me her father suffered from chronic hiccups and her mother would often take refuge in Judy's bedroom to get some sleep. Her car was in the driveway that night because Judy's Dad was planning to work on it the next day.

I don't know if it was to show remorse for my bad-boy behavior or mere curiosity, but I was now attending church often with Judy and her parents on Sundays when she was home on weekends. I had to admit that I was impressed by Judy, the Foxes, and several of Judy's friends at UNT who attended her Intervarsity Christian Fellowship meetings. They all seemed to have an authenticity and genuine care for me that I had not found in fellow Muslims.

Occasionally, I joined the Foxes on Sundays even when Judy wasn't home. I was confused by many things I was learning. The Jesus of the Bible seemed far different than the prophet I had been raised to believe Him to be. I enjoyed singing songs in church, because I could comprehend the words. In Islam, most of the reading and praying is in Arabic, a language few people in Pakistan speak and understand. I was drawn to this community that loved me even though I wasn't one of them.

Although it had only been four months since Judy and I had met, it felt like we'd known each other much longer. The quality of our time together had been so rich. I had been seeing Judy exclusively for the past several months. Gone were the days of fooling around.

In Pakistan, even to this day most marriages are arranged. For middle to upper-income families, although some dating goes on, the quality and quantity of time is limited at best. Couples may be allowed to go to a restaurant, talk on the phone, or go to the beach or a park, but parents, brothers, and uncles are always on the watch, not to mention law-enforcement, depending on which Muslim country you are in. The freedom, especially for women, to meet and get to know the person they are expected to spend the rest of their lives with, is highly restricted.

Prior to 2003, a Pakistani bride age eighteen or older was not even granted the right to marry a person of her own choosing (free-will marriage) without the consent of her guardians.[23] That says it all for the freedom of love in my home country. Still, despite such laws being on the books, honor killings are not unheard of, even to this day, in rural Pakistan. Honor killings are a way for the male members of the family, usually the father or the older brother, to vindicate the perceived shame brought onto the family by the actions of the girl. Love has a high cost in the Muslim world.

Although I have briefly touched earlier on the Pakistani matrimonial process, it bodes elaborating. The average middle-class marriage process looks like this: a young man goes to an event such as a wedding, with or without his family, where girls are adorned in beautiful make-up, henna, jewelry and colorful dresses with ornate handiwork. He might flirt with a girl who is a friend of a relative. They might even interact at several events—a single Pakistani wedding has no shortage of gatherings and festivities.

At some point over the coming weeks or months, the boy informs his mother or aunt of his interest in the girl, after which a research process about the family and the girl would be initiated.

"It's all about the family," Ammi used to say. "If the family is good, *Beta*, then the girl will be good too."

This assumption, in and of itself, can have disastrous consequences, as one might imagine.

A proposal is eventually lobbed to the other side. If the girl's side responds affirmatively, the boy's side is invited to *chai* (tea) at the girl's home so that her parents can meet him, and his parents can see the girl in an official capacity. This "viewing" is often conducted by asking her to bring the tea and samosas/sweets into the room where everyone is seated.

A brief question-and-answer ensues. For the girl, the questions tend to be related to her studies, hobbies, and so forth. For the boy, the questions center around his qualifications, job and income. The boy's family, especially if he is from a higher-income bracket, has the upper-hand in these discussions. After all, the girl is the one with the clock ticking over her head. Heaven forbid that a wrinkle or two appear or she gain a few extra pounds before she is married. Pakistani parents these days are so paranoid about such factors that over half the girls are wed before the age of eighteen.[24]

In addition, there is also the enormous burden of a dowry. According to custom, Pakistani brides must be accompanied by a variety of material assets: furniture, jewelry, and so on, to please the groom's family and warrant respectful treatment. The lower down the economic food chain one goes, the less chance a bride has of even meeting the man she will marry prior to the ceremony.

> *I was grateful to America for granting me the freedom to get to know the one I believed I loved. She could choose to accept or reject me of her own accord.*

Although the girl is generally the party most impacted by this lack of freedom, many Pakistani young men also face extreme pressure to select a bride in a manner akin to picking from a lineup. The goal, to cement ties between two strong families and bring economic advantage, often opens the door to rampant nepotism. Good jobs are often given to relatives to keep the power and wealth within the two families.

As I walked in a park one evening with Judy, I was grateful to America for granting me the freedom to get to know the one I believed I loved. She could choose to accept or reject me of her own accord. Nevertheless, I understood that familial, cultural, and socio-economic pressures could play a role in a woman's choice for a mate in America. I had, on more than one occasion, heard Judy say, "When you marry someone, you marry their whole family." And, as I was soon to discover, faith also could play a major role.

I don't know what spurred me to blurt out those three little words that night. Perhaps for me, four months was plenty long, given the context. I knew Judy was the one.

"I love you," I said to her.

Silence.

After what felt like an hour, she said, "I…I don't know what to say. I am not prepared to say that back to you at this point."

I was confused and felt like a fool.

She's wrong. She'll change her mind.

That is how my sanguine brain worked. It was how I'd survived all those years, focusing on the good and the positive.

As we drove home in silence, I assured myself that she would change her mind. Judy thought we both needed a break. I wasn't on board, but I didn't want the whole thing to melt down, either, so I agreed.

"Come to Denton and attend church with me. I think you will love the pastor there. He used to be a quarterback at UNT."

She was right. Tommy Nelson was a young pastor in his late thirties, charismatic and handsome. The church was full of young college students and young men who were totally engaged with God. The energy in the room was magnetic. Nelson taught directly from the Bible and the topic that first Sunday, providentially perhaps, was "Finding Your Mate." I was amazed by the sermon and wanted to learn more about this God of the Bible.

Judy and I continued to see each other, but now just weekly, pretending the three words I had uttered didn't change anything. We spoke more about spiritual things.

"What does Islam say about this?" she would ask, referring to whatever topic we were discussing.

I got defensive at times, trying to explain. Most of the time, I didn't have an answer. I started to study the Quran, the Muslim holy book, to find them. I had Ammi's English version of the Quran, but I found reading it to be a rather mind-numbing undertaking. The book is not organized like a narrative story nor is it chronological. The reading felt like a compilation of authoritarian statements to me.

This was the first time in my life that I had Scripture in easy-to-understand English. I found its words jumping out at me. I was drawn to it like a moth to a flame, except I wasn't feeling the burn. Only love.

My birthday came in August and Judy planned an elaborate scavenger hunt, complete with rhyming clues and small gifts hidden all over Arlington—reminders of our relationship. One of the final clues, neatly written on a notepad that had a cow on it, led me to the local bookstore. All I was permitted to say to the clerk was, "Bessie sent me."

Looking and feeling foolish, I followed the instructions. Much to my relief, the salesman at the store understood my coded message.

"This is for you," he said, grinning and handing me a wrapped-up book. I opened the wrapping and inside was a Bible with my name printed on it.

I spent much of that week reading it. This was the first time in my life that I had Scripture in easy-to-understand English. I found its words jumping out at me. I was drawn to it like a moth to a flame, except I wasn't feeling the burn. Only love.

One day, Rahim walked in on me as I was reading, and it was as if I had been rudely awakened from a deep sleep. I shook my head and reminded myself that I was a bona-fide Muslim. I decided then and there that the solution was to convert Judy to Islam.

She would make an outstanding Muslim wife.

I started to study both the Quran and the Bible side-by-side to work up a strategy.

Judy and I often spoke into the wee hours of the night. We didn't argue; we mostly explored principles. I remember her walking me through the concept of grace.

"It's like someone has invited you to eat a delicious dinner of steak and potatoes. But it's entirely up to you whether to accept it or not," she said.

I understood this analogy since Steak & Ale was one of our favorite restaurants, but I was struggling with the idea of grace. Islam is all about works. You must earn your salvation through praying five times a day, going on a pilgrimage, giving alms, fasting, and so forth.[25] Once again, I was intrigued by what I was convinced was completely new and radical information, something not previously taught to me.

I quickly realized my visions of converting Judy into a good Muslim wife were a pipe dream. Even more disturbing, it was clear that Judy, John, Jean, the pastor, and others in Judy's InterVarsity group were living out the grace-filled lifestyle I read about in the Bible. They were kind not only to me but to each other. They were other-centered and winsome. They also seem to have this other common attribute—joy. This was all very unsettling.

I went to the mosque that Friday, hoping for some clarity. However, I couldn't invite Judy to come with me. In Muslim culture, women usually don't go to the mosque. When they do, they generally sit in a separate section from the men. I needed to speak with Allah about all that was going on, but praying behind a group of men, all chanting Arabic verses relayed by the Imam, did not settle my heart.

I was feeling conflicted. I felt love for Judy, but guilt at how I was feeling about my faith, not to mention frustration for not being able to figure out how I could have it both ways. I suspected that Judy and I were coming to a crossroads.

My intuition was correct. Judy had purchased tickets to an Amy Grant concert that was in town. Grant was one of the most popular Christian singers in those days. Unbeknownst to me, Judy received a phone call earlier that week from her childhood friend, Sully. Judy had gushed to her about the time she was spending with me.

"What exactly do you think you are doing, dating a non-Christian?" Sully asked in her usual blunt style.

Defensive, Judy responded, "I am not *dating* a Muslim. We just do things together."

"Call it what you like, but you're going out. You *are* dating him." Sully replied.

Though offended, Judy realized that Sully was right to call her out on this. She and I were clearly in what the Bible called an "unequally-yoked" relationship.[26]

"You have to break this off, you know." Sully's tone was softer now.

Judy got quiet as she pondered this. She thanked her friend for calling and promised to speak later. She had to get ready for our concert date.

I was an hour late to the concert that night, busy buying a new shirt and not planning for the horrific downtown traffic. In hindsight, choosing to look good over being timely was a foolish mistake to make with a girl who believed punctuality was a respect issue. It proved to be fatal.

When I arrived at the venue, Judy was waiting for me—fuming. I had never seen her this angry.

"Here." she said. Tears ran down her cheeks as she stretched out her hand with my ticket, so I could get in through the turnstile. Then, she spun around and stalked off to her seat. I followed, sheepishly. Neither of us spoke a word during the entire concert. Her face was sad and serious.

Way to go, Casanova.

On the drive back, she took control of the conversation over my repeated apologies. "I'm going to make a bad evening worse," she said, keeping her tone steady.

I braced myself.

"I can't see you anymore." Her voice was now quivering.

"But why? I'm sorry for being late to the concert," I pleaded.

"It's not the concert. It's us. We can't do this. You are a Muslim and I am a Christian, and relationships have to go somewhere." She was now crying as she spoke.

I blurted out, "Okay, okay, I was going to tell you this at Christmas as a gift, but I'll tell you now: I have decided to become a Christian."

Silence hung in the air while what I had just uttered sunk in. I had never dreamed of saying that up to this point. It was like an out-of-body experience for me. I wanted to step outside myself and say, "You are gonna do *what*? Did you say what I just heard you say?"

In hindsight, I clearly didn't understand what I was saying. Looking back, there was an irony to it. I offered my conversion as a Christmas gift to her when it was I who would receive the greatest gift to be bestowed on mankind—salvation.

I don't want to minimize the power of the words, "I have decided to become a Christian," and how much blurting those words out changed the landscape for me. However, I was not thinking about a genuine conversion. In my culture, it wasn't unusual for men or women to convert on paper simply to marry the one they love. A Shia man might agree to become a Sunni, for example, to appease the girl's Sunni family. Such conversions weren't a reality of the heart, but the act of saying one had converted made the relationship acceptable.

It was at this moment that our damsel-in-distress made the wisest decision she knew to make on behalf of our relationship, albeit one-sided from my standpoint. "Well, if that's true, then that's fabulous, Ali. Best decision you've ever made. I think you and God need to get to know each other one-on-one."

"Oh, no. I think I can do both." I said in desperation. "I can get to know you and God at the same time."

She shook her head. "I'm sorry, but I don't think that would be a good idea." She was resolved.

Tears ran down my cheeks as we pulled into the UNT parking lot. We hugged and cried and said what we both thought was our last goodbye.

As I drove in silence back to Arlington, my thoughts ran back to Seemi, a neighborhood girl in Karachi I barely knew but was infatuated with. Days before I departed for the States, I remember urging my father to take a marriage proposal over to her house.

Abboo talked me out of it. "You are going to meet someone later in life, Son," he said in his gentle, kind voice.

Now, having lost the woman I loved, I momentarily longed for the simplicity of an arranged marriage.

It would be so easy. Especially now that I'm branded as a return-from-America.

Those depressing thoughts passed by the time I tucked myself into bed.

No, "Tis better to have loved and lost…"

My final thought before I slid into an emotionally-exhausted slumber was of what Judy had said to me.

You and God need to get to know each other….

I leaned over to switch off the lamp and saw my gift from Judy lying on the nightstand.

The Bible was calling my name.

Chapter 7

FREEDOM OF RELIGION PART I: FREEDOM TO SEEK THE TRUTH

The chanting grew louder and wilder by the minute.

"Ya Hussain! Ya Hussain! Ya Hussain!"

Shirtless men beat their chests in a rhythmic motion, fists rising in sync and slamming hard against their hairy chests.

From atop Uncle Imran's shoulders, I had a clear view of the entire scene. I was mesmerized by one muscular and bearded man whose chest was bleeding. Our eyes met for a moment as the bearded man gave his chest a small cut, tossed his razor aside, and continued this annual ritual of *Matham*. Other sights were gorier still. Men were using the *zanjeer*, an instrument with small knives attached to a chain, used to beat one's back.

Uncle Imran kept us at a safe distance lest one of the knives fly loose and hit us. Anyone dying during this gruesome tradition would be considered a martyr.

It was quite a sight for a twelve-year-old to witness, but I was in good company. Children even younger than I, dressed all in black, roamed about with their fathers and uncles. Women stayed out of the way but were actively engaged in their own gatherings of mourning, called *Majlis*. My mother was in high demand during these times. She had a beautiful voice and sang songs of mourning at these meetings.

The most prominent differences between the minority Shia Muslims like me, who are mostly found in Iran and Iraq, and the majority Sunni community that dominates the Muslim world are the traditions of *Muharram*. This is where Shias the world-over mourn the martyrdom of Hussain, the grandson of Muhammed, the son of the revered Caliph Imam Ali, Muhammed's son-in-law.[27] *Matham* is the practice of invoking Hussain's memory.

99

Such was the household in which I grew up. Ammi, my mother, taught me much about Islam and Shiism. Every wall in our home was adorned with proud Shia symbols and prayers written in beautiful Arabic calligraphy. There were the words, "Ya Ali" in gold lettering. In our prayer room hung a huge picture of pilgrims circling the *Kaaba*, the center of Islam located in Mecca, Saudi Arabia, where Muslims from across the globe go to perform the *Haj* (pilgrimage). Being a Shia is an entire identity and a way of life. You are not separate from it.

As I considered reading the Bible seriously for the first time, those thoughts filled my head. I feared what I might discover if I read the Bible without prejudice, not knowing where it might lead me. Yet I was compelled to do it. I had seen and heard too much. I had met enough people who called themselves Christians that I respected. And I had heard enough messages preached on Sundays that explained the emptiness I felt. It did not align with the worldview in which I'd been raised.

Thanks to the freedoms available to me in the United States, I believed I had stumbled upon information that warranted closer examination. In Texas I did not risk the kind of persecution I most assuredly would face in Pakistan. And now, thanks to Judy's decision to part ways with me, I felt no compulsion to pursue this path for her sake. As much as it hurt me to think it, I knew she was right.

You and God need to get to know one another.

Her voice echoed in my head.

It had been several months since we parted ways. After our break-up, I languished in my apartment for days, lashing out in anger at Rahim when he tried to console me. Finally, I returned to my old ways of partying and rang up Josie, but nothing felt the same. Every word she uttered sounded shallow. I poured myself into work. Judy was back at school and no longer working at the store. I doubted she would choose to work there again the next summer.

I came home one day to find an envelope in the mailbox addressed in her beautiful penmanship. I tore it open, my heart racing. It was a kind note. She was thinking of and praying for me. She talked about her school and her upcoming Art Appreciation final. She asked about my progress at North Lake and about our mutual acquaintances at the store.

I frowned at her friendly but respectfully distant tone.

"Gotta run. Will write more soon. Drop me a note when you can."

I felt sad. UNT was only an hour drive, but she felt a thousand miles away. I noticed a verse reference on the bottom of the card: Philippians 1:3. I snatched up the Bible and opened to the alphabetical index. Turning to the verse, I read, "I thank my God every time I remember you."

How amazing, I thought, that such an appropriate verse could be found in Scripture that was written two thousand years ago.

By now, after carefully comparing the Quran and the Bible, I had given up on the notion that the Bible was corrupted as Muslim scholars taught and Ammi reinforced. That seemed a convenient argument, without much foundation and easily debunked by many independent Western scholars.

This was to be a spiritual verdict, and the weights and measures used were not to be found in any apologetics book or science lab. This was an affair of the heart, and my soul and its eternal destiny hung in the balance.

Leaving aside the fact that the Bible resonated and spoke to my heart every time I opened it, even rudimentary research showed me that there were numerous manuscripts of the Bible discovered long before the emergence of Islam in 610 A.D.[28] For every book the Arlington mosque library contained about the veracity of the Quran and the fallacy of the Bible, there were at least three well-written books in the UTA library that defended the Bible. Research showed that, compared to other ancient documents, the Bible was the most authentic thing going. And while there were many translations—a common objection taught to young Muslims like me—they virtually all described the same events with only minor variations.[29]

However, the challenge before me was not strictly academic. It was far more serious. This was to be a spiritual verdict, and the weights and measures used were not to be found in any apologetics book or science lab. This was an affair of the heart, and my soul and its eternal destiny hung in the balance.

To further my quest, I had been sneaking off to attend church on Sunday mornings and landed at Pantego Bible Church. The pastor was preaching from the book of Mark, Chapter 8. The sermon was titled, "The Identity of Christ." The question Jesus asked Peter hit me squarely in the face.

"'But what about you?' [Jesus] asked. 'Who do you say that I am?'" Peter had answered correctly—the Messiah.[30]

Growing up in Pakistan, attending Cathedral High School, and being served by many Catholic servants, I had always heard of *Isa Masih* (the Urdu name for Jesus). But I had never thought about what *Masih* or Messiah meant. Now, that seemed to be the central question. Who did *I* think He was? I made an earnest decision to figure it out for myself.

Growing up in a strong Muslim household, I was fully convinced Islam was the only true, final, and complete religion. In fact, as a Shia Muslim, we were further taught that most of the Muslim world took a detour by not choosing to follow the leadership of my namesake, Imam Ali.[31]

"Never mind," Ammi always said. At the end of time, the Twelfth Imam and Jesus would return to earth to lead all unbelievers, other "people of the Book" (i.e. Jews and Christians) and those Muslims who had diverged in their theology, back to the straight-and-narrow path of Shia Islam.

Religion dominated our lives. There were rules about everything in Islam, from how to pray to how to use the bathroom. Many of my cousins had read the Quran from cover to cover, a badge of honor and cause for celebration by the family, as was fasting during the day for the entire month of *Ramadan*.

My best friend Jamal was a Sunni. We looked forward to *Ramadan* each year, not for the spiritual value of it, but for the opportunity to play cricket all day and then eating all the goodies at sunset when the entire Muslim world broke its fast. My father was a compliant Muslim but not as engaged in his faith as my mother. I don't recall him teaching me anything religious; I learned from my mother. But even with her, the focus was on the ritual itself, not why it existed. My Islamic studies book said that fasting occurred so one could empathize with the less fortunate, but the reality was that by fasting I could earn *sawab* (good works credit).

Although some of my cousins progressed along this production-based holiness curve, I didn't feel attracted to it. Something was missing. Besides, Ammi always emphasized that I would experience a magical transformation at the age of forty, just as Muhammed did.[32] Then, I could focus more fully on religion. The religiosity of my faith left me with a void I could not clearly identify.

To be clear, I don't for a single moment mean that I was not interested in God, doubted His existence, or His authority. But the notion of a personal relationship with God is not a concept taught in Islam, at least not in the circles in which I traveled. Still, long before Judy exposed me to the radical concept of having a relationship with the living God, I felt a desire to journal to Allah. I even wrote a few times to Imam Ali, and it felt strangely right to do so. Even the idea of loving others wasn't foreign to me.

One day when I was fifteen, I woke up with a burning desire in my heart to love people. I remember immediately getting up, opening my writing desk, and making a list of all the boys in my neighborhood that I needed to unconditionally love. That, I believed, was the key to living a good life. I have no idea where these urges originated. The very first name on the list, Wasim, was a neighbor and about my age. He was uncouth, argumentative, average-looking, and a mediocre cricket player. He fit my difficult-to-love category. My experiment in love failed miserably. I couldn't even get past Wasim. I thought about him as I read the Beatitudes from the book of Matthew: "Blessed are the poor in spirit, for theirs is the kingdom of heaven."[33]

What a contrast.

To claim spirituality in Shia Islam, you had to earn it, perhaps graduate from a *Madrasa* and then go to Islamic school in Qom, Iran, to become an Ayatollah.[34]

I read on. "Blessed are those who hunger and thirst for righteousness, for they will be filled."[35]

I thought back to the young college students like Judy at the church back in Denton, all well under the age of forty. They were not there out of obligation. They craved something deeper. Was it righteousness? What did it mean to be righteous?

"Blessed are the merciful, for they will be shown mercy."[36]

This focus on non-ritualistic behavior was not wasted on me. Jesus modeled it by how He dealt with the sick, the poor, the downtrodden, the children, and even sinners.

I finished reading the entire Gospel of Matthew and was drawn to the figure of Christ. I had a hard time imagining Him being a liar. His agenda seemed completely altruistic. He showed no desire for earthly power, no battles or conquests, no sex, and no caliphate, yet He spoke as one with unequivocal authority. In Luke 19, he said, "The Son of Man came to seek and to save the lost."[37] That was His mission, His prime directive.

"Am I lost?" I wondered out loud.

I certainly felt it.

The deeper I read into the story of Christ, the more truth I felt oozing out of the book I was reading, and the more shocked I was about the amount of misinformation I had been given all my life

I had been taught from a young age that Jesus never died, but that Allah faked Jesus' death by putting someone else on the cross. But here, and many other places in both the Old and New Testament, it was clearly prophesied that the Messiah would save His people and that He would indeed die.[38] In fact, Jesus predicted His own death multiple times.[39]

In Matthew 20, responding to two disciples who sought favored status in the coming kingdom, Jesus said whoever wanted to be first in God's eyes must be willing to be last. He told them that even He, the promised King and Messiah, did not come to earth to be served, but rather to serve and to give His life as a ransom for many.[40]

That night after my shift was over, I picked up the Bible once more. As I continued scanning the Gospels, a passage in John 15 resonated with me. Jesus was making an analogy of a vine and its branches. He had an amazing way of teaching. I found myself increasingly thirsty for His words:

"Remain in me, as I also remain in you. No branch can bear fruit by itself; it must remain in the vine. Neither can you bear fruit unless you remain in me. I am the vine; you are the branches. If you remain in me and I in you, you will bear much fruit; apart from me you can do nothing."[41]

My thoughts ran back to my failed experiment with Wasim and others in Karachi. Could it be, I pondered, my idea had been good, even righteous, but I was connected to the wrong power source? Deep down in my heart, I was afraid. I turned the lamp off but lay awake thinking about my discoveries. There was absolutely no family member I could talk to about this. They would think I was insane.

Both Rahim and Josie noticed my new-found obsession. I was going to school, working, and then reading the Bible. For his part, thankfully, Rahim was still friendly, as he was not a serious Muslim. "Just be careful, man," he would say when he would see me engrossed in my reading.

Josie's reactions were more visceral. "What in the hell did Judy tell you?" Josie demanded. "I'm a damn Baptist, for heaven's sake. I could help you with your questions."

"No, I don't think you can," I said, slowly shaking my head and wondering if she saw the irony of her words.

I bet she doesn't even know the difference between the Old and New Testament.

Josie served as an important reminder, that both faiths could have poor representatives. By now, I had experienced the vast difference between those who were "Sunday Christians," like Josie and my ex-girlfriend Lindsey, and folks like the Foxes who put their Christian faith into action. I also learned that there were big theological differences between mainstream protestant Christianity, which the Foxes followed, and other faiths that I had previously tagged as all being Christian.

That was another item I added to my list of what I found amazing about America. Information was readily available for anyone who wished to examine it. I could go to any public library, and it was rich in its collection of perspectives on just about any topic. I just needed a library card. Books about the history of the Bible, prophesy, errors in the Bible, science and the Bible, and much more were all there to be explored. I marveled at this freedom to privately seek, search, and study whatever I chose. There were no restrictions. I didn't need to hide. No "big brother" was watching over my shoulder ready to report me to the authorities. Nor did the government control which books the libraries could issue to the interested reader.

Over the next few months, I read through all four Gospels and was intellectually convinced that the Bible I held in my hand was the truth, and that Jesus was a lot more than a prophet. I was equally convinced that much misinformation existed about him in the Muslim world. But what was I supposed to do with all this information? How did I fit? More importantly, where did Islam fit?

"You should read the book of Romans. I think it might help," the nice librarian lady had told me, smiling. She wore a pretty, gold chain around her neck with a cross on it.

I thanked her as I left, intrigued by her recommendation.

I took two weeks off from the store, using all my accumulated vacation time. Rahim had gone back to Pakistan to visit his family and I had our apartment to myself. I studied the book of Romans over those fourteen days.

I cannot pinpoint exactly which day during those two weeks the cosmic shift between head-knowledge and heart-acceptance occurred, but it did. Perhaps it happened when I read and understood Romans 3, where it explains that everyone (including yours truly) has fallen short of God's perfect standard. Or when I read that righteousness comes only through faith and not works or observance of law—an upside-down concept for a Muslim who lives each day under the burden of law.

Or, perhaps I believed when I understood in Chapter 6 that sin is not merely external, as Islam portrays it, but is an internal corruption that requires, no, *demands* redemption before a Holy God. The alternative is death—the eternal kind.

I didn't feel angry when reading in Chapter 5 that this corrupt condition of mine entered the world through Adam and that my sin nature was not something I created. It was innate. The mantra of "I'm a good person" was insufficient. If I was going to be honest with myself, measuring by the standards I had seen lived out and taught by Christ, I had to admit that my heart's desires were ignoble at best.

The same chapters that laid out my sin predicament also clearly explained the antidote for my deteriorating condition: Christ's perfect sacrifice on my behalf and His love poured out for me.

For a Muslim, becoming a follower of Christ is a long and often-hazardous process that can span many months, if not years. However, conversion of any soul is an event.

As I read Romans, everything clicked. My heart beat faster with every chapter. The best way I know to describe it was this: all those moments growing up where I felt close to a higher power, all those times when I prayed thinking someone was listening, all those feelings when Islamic rituals felt hollow but talking to the Creator didn't. They all started to make sense. The many dots of my life had connected to form a picture.

It was like, *Oh, so you're the one that has been with me all my life. Orchestrating things. Protecting me. Nudging me to press on and not give up. And bringing me all the way here to the United States. Nice to finally meet you, Jesus.*

The next gate I needed to pass through lay before me. I must believe. I didn't need holy water sprinkled over me. I didn't need a priest reading from a book in a language I could not comprehend. I didn't even need to go to a church.

For a Muslim, becoming a follower of Christ is a long and often-hazardous process that can span many months, if not years. However, conversion of any soul is an event. Sitting alone in that Arlington apartment, it was a simple prayer to Jesus, thanking him for his atoning death on my behalf and asking him to take the reins of my life into his hands, forgiving me for my sin and leading me wherever he wanted me to go.

Who did I think he was? He was my Savior. And this time, it was for real.

Of course, at this juncture I had no idea that dreadful and dark forces stood ready to oppose me. I didn't begin this perilous journey of faith thinking Islam was wrong. I just knew, based on my own experience and analysis, that its representation of Christ was incomplete and that I had to follow Him—with or without Judy. I felt defenseless against His love.

It was that simple.

In his second letter to the Corinthian church, the apostle Paul wrote, "Anyone who belongs to Christ is a new person. The past is forgotten, and everything is new."[42] I am one of the few Muslim-background believers I know of who did not have a supernatural encounter, such as a dream or vision, or hear an audible voice during my spiritual journey. However, the immediate and tangible changes I experienced the moment I trusted Jesus were equally compelling evidence of the supernatural.

First, my language changed. Gone were my "f-bombs." When I played racquetball with Rahim later that month, "Oh, shoot!" was the best I could muster when I missed my drop shot. That caused Rahim to raise an eyebrow.

My habits, desires, motivations, treatment of others, and attitudes all changed rapidly. I felt an uncanny desire to tell the truth, but it wasn't to earn any credit with God now. I wanted to be pure in His eyes simply to please him. I knew Jesus was watching even if no one else was. In fact, He was coaching me moment-by-moment. The Bible was still the instruction manual, but prayer was now a means of communication. I felt inexpressible peace and joy. I was in awe that things written two thousand years ago were impacting my daily interactions.

It wasn't that I had been transformed into someone perfect. Far from it. What was different was that now there were both temptations to sin and opportunities to honor Christ, along with conviction when I failed to do so. An entirely new spiritual dimension opened to me.

My co-workers, classmates, and some of the UTA InterVarsity group members noticed the changes. I still attended their Bible studies, and they were my one indirect connection to Judy, since she was a member of the UNT chapter.

The other group taking note of the changes in my life was my family in the DFW area. I decided not to keep my decision a secret should the right opportunity present itself. No one had taught me how to share the message of Jesus in any sort of sensitive or contextualized way. I had been exposed to Christianity in a highly Western style, which suited me just fine. However, I never considered that perhaps that approach might be offensive to my family.

I quickly realized if I was to be authentic about my beliefs, hiding the kind of dynamic spiritual metamorphosis I was undergoing was next to impossible. Muslim family members can be both bossy and nosy, especially when it comes to ensuring that their younger relatives remain on the straight and narrow path.

"So, are you going to the mosque for Friday prayers with the other men?" asked Nazneen. The other men she referred to were her husband and her brother as well as Jamshed, my uncle's son.

I did not feel like I could go to Friday prayers with the guys. However, I also didn't want to give the impression to my cousins that I didn't care about praying.

"No, not today."

"Ali, praying is important. It's a key way you earn *sawab* (credit)," Nazneen said.

Okay, here goes nothing.

"It's not that I don't want to pray," I said. "I pray all the time. In fact, it's one of the main ways I talk to and hear from God. I just don't pray the same way I used to." I let the words hang in the air as I looked straight into her eyes.

That was how it started. What I had given her was a very unorthodox remark. It would have been vastly easier to make up an excuse such as having an important errand to run, a study group to attend, or some other dog-ate-my-homework equivalent for not being able to make the all-important Friday prayers. I could have even told her I intended to pray *qaza* (make-up prayers), a convenient instrument in Islam that allows a follower to run a credit balance with Allah.

Nazneen, and later my cousins and her husband, pounced on my response with a litany of questions. I ended up sharing with them about my discoveries about Jesus, and they immediately rebutted with the standard objections that I, too, had been taught. Indeed, the same ones I would have raised myself only months ago: Jesus was only a prophet. Mohammed was the greatest prophet sent by Allah. The Bible is totally corrupt. The Quran is the perfect word of Allah, and so on.

I tried to stay calm. Fortunately, we were in America, in a modern apartment complex with neighbors on all sides. And all four of my relatives were well-educated, modern Muslims. Such a conversation in a village in Pakistan would probably have ended quickly, with me going to the hospital—or the morgue.

"You are so confused." Nazneen said with a finality that indicated the debate was over. "I don't know what *jaadoo* (voodoo) Judy has done on you, but *Khaala* will fix you up."

Khaala means aunt in Urdu, and this was no ordinary aunt. This was my mother. All the nieces and nephews were sent to her for answers to complex questions about Islam. My cousins' consensus was that I was confused, deliriously in love, and must talk with Ammi, who would straighten out my errant theology with effortless ease and expediency. It would be game—set—match.

In the interim, they arranged for an appointment with the local imam at the mosque. We spoke from nine in the evening until one in the morning. The conversation was civil because we were in the United States. The single most astonishing thing I remember from that conversation, even thirty years later, was that the imam genuinely believed that a person could live a sinless life on earth. I did not believe that, and it was a fundamental difference between us. I believed we all desperately need a savior, because we are corrupt at the core. He pointed to his own good works in anticipation of standing before a just and pure God. After four hours of debate, I left with my exhausted cousin.

Later in my spiritual journey, I learned how improbable it would be for a young person like me to have such a conversation with an imam and still be allowed to leave the mosque without citing the *Shahada* ("There is no god but Allah and Mohammed is his messenger"). As a modern Muslim, I was quickly learning that although it was nominally okay for me to have questions, it was absolutely unacceptable for me to forsake Islam. Converting to Christianity was apostasy, plain and simple.

My head was spinning as I drove home from the mosque. How did I go from normal to apostate? Why was it so wrong for me to believe in God in this new way?

A relative of mine believed the changes in my beliefs and actions were so serious that they took it upon themselves to record a cassette tape of all my recent misdeeds: dating a Christian girl, going to church, reading the Bible, skipping Friday prayers, and sent it to my parents. Of course, they didn't mention in their report that I'd stopped cussing and drinking, that I didn't lie anymore, and I no longer skipped classes.

The seriousness of all this was finally sinking in. My most intimate of choices—what I believed about my Creator— mattered to an entire community.

I felt horribly betrayed. *I'd* wanted to be the one to tell my parents. I wanted them to understand what I'd come to believe and that they hadn't failed me. Now I was on the phone, half a world away, trying to explain myself over a scratchy connection. How does one even begin to communicate what I had experienced? What I remember the most about that conversation with my loving parents was the unmistakable pain in their voices and my mother's surreal response when I asked her if I was in danger from my extended family if I returned to Karachi.

"Well, *Beta*, they belong to you and you belong to them."

Abboo proposed we meet in Turkey, which had a reputation for being a modern Muslim country. The seriousness of all this was finally sinking in. My most intimate of choices—what I believed about my Creator—mattered to an entire community.

After hanging up I felt an overwhelming sense of deep loss: the loss of my parents. It was as if they were there, yet they were gone. I could no longer rely on their wisdom. I felt their views had a shallowness to them I had not previously noticed. Their thoughts were not influenced by Christ nor based on what I now viewed as the Word of God.

Weeks flew by, and I continued rapidly along a spiritual growth curve, drawn by what I now knew to be inexplicable forces. I was amazed by the daily guidance, answers, and reassurances I found in my Scripture readings. Some of the answers were not pleasant in the short-term. I learned in the book of Mark that even Jesus' own family ridiculed him when he spoke of a new spiritual order: "When his family heard about this, they went to take charge of him, for they said, 'He is out of his mind.'"[43]

In that same passage, Jesus also pointed me to my new family and parents: "'Who are my mother and my brothers?' He asked. Then he looked at those seated in a circle around him and said. 'Here are my mother and my brothers! Whoever does God's will is my brother and sister and mother.'"[44]

My reading foreshadowed things to come. Hard things. Painful things. Ultimately, the verses that gave me the greatest sense of both consternation and purpose lay in the tenth chapter of Matthew. Jesus was sending out his twelve disciples to the people of Israel with a series of instructions and, although they were empowered to bring blessing and healing, Jesus told them they would be persecuted: "You will be hated by everyone because of me...."[45] I understood that this message, though given two thousand years ago to the disciples, also applied to me.

But why, Jesus? Aren't the disciples (and now me) the good guys?

Jesus pointed out, "The student is not above the teacher, nor a servant above his master. It is enough for students to be like their teachers, and servants like their masters."[46] In other words, if they didn't spare me, why do you expect them to spare you? There was no equivocation. The choice was clear. You either followed Jesus all the way to the end or you didn't. And, if that meant picking up your own cross, so be it. You could either save your temporary earthly life, or you could opt for life eternal with Him.

Dang. This theme of sacrifice, suffering, and the need for courage is everywhere.

This didn't feel or sound at all like the fun Sunday church services I had been attracted to, where everyone was smiling, dressed nicely, and enjoyed huge potlucks after the sermon. American churches didn't discuss the cost of following Jesus much.

In cricket terms, Jesus had just bowled me a *googly*. This is when a batsman facing a ball from the bowler expects the ball to bounce and turn left, but instead it goes the other way.

Am I up to this challenge?

I didn't know the answer.

What I did know was that I needed to find a community of like-minded folks—my brothers and my mother, as Jesus had called them. I invested myself into the InterVarsity Christian Fellowship (I.V.) chapter of UT Arlington. They welcomed me with open arms and became my new family.

At times, I.V. chapters from different schools would hold joint events. One weekend, students from various campuses statewide were to serve dinner to the adult InterVarsity staff as thanks for their service on college campuses throughout Texas. I thought about the possibility of running into Judy and questions buzzed through my brain. Had she missed me as much as I had missed her? Would she see me as the changed person I had become? Was she seeing someone?

I didn't like to think about that last question.

We ran into each other in the parking lot after the dinner concluded. Judy had served as a babysitter for the staff's children and I had been a waiter. Several of her friends had already updated her about my changed condition, and she was thrilled for me and my growing faith.

I offered to drive her back to her campus, which gave us the opportunity to catch up. No, she was not seeing anyone. Yes, she was going to be home for the summer. And yes, she would love to go on a date with me.

Perhaps I was being overzealous, but I now had an ally in the Holy Spirit and I fully planned to consult with Him on how to handle things the right way this go-round. That summer, Judy and I were once again inseparable as she and her parents got to know the new me.

I noticed another change in how people related to me. Everywhere I went in Christian circles, I was a novelty. People wanted to hear my testimony as a former Muslim. It inspired them, and I believe it reaffirmed their own faith. I became adept at telling my story. Bible churches in North Texas operated like well-oiled machines, so often I had only four to six minutes between the last worship song and the sermon to share my story. I much preferred the Sunday school question-and-answer format that followed my testimony, where I could interact directly with the audience. It felt natural and right, and I loved it. Here I was, a mere thirty-six months removed from living a life surrounded by the rites and rituals of Shia Islam, and now I was speaking in front of hundreds of most-ly-Caucasian audiences in churches across Texas, answering questions about my conversion to Christianity. It was surreal.

I enjoyed being in front of these large crowds, making them laugh, answering their many questions, and sharing my new-found insights. In fact, I began to feel guilty. Was I enjoying it all a bit too much? Was my head bloating? Was this for God or for my own sake? I discussed this with Paisley, one of Judy's cousins, who also was a practicing Christian.

"We rarely ever do anything one hundred percent for God," she told me. "There is always some part of our selfish self that we are fighting. You are okay. It's natural to feel this conflict."

I remember appreciating those comments. This was a process and I had a lot to learn.

As it turns out, I had much to learn about being in a Christian dating relationship. Now that I was a Christian man, I thought it was my responsibility to lead. All the I.V. talks on Christian dating I'd heard said the man should be the leader. I erroneously interpreted that to mean that the man must make all the decisions. I should have known that this would not go over well with the very independent and opinionated Judy.

Tension between us grew all summer as I tried to be "the man" by throwing out unsolicited spiritual advice, having all the answers during the I.V. Bible studies, and using as many big theological terms as possible. This threw the balance of our relationship off its center. There were times when I was just myself and we had fun together like before. But often I was hiding behind a façade. You could see the train wreck coming a mile away.

I had moved in with a new roommate whom I met at InterVarsity summer camp. John aspired to be a missionary in China and teach English, and I admired his maturity. Like John, most of the guys at camp seemed far ahead of me. They were white, had grown up in the church, and had the support of Christian parents. There were, of course, some misfits. I ran into men with complex and broken lives, but lives on which Christ had made a visible impact. I wanted badly to jump to the front of the maturity line without those life experiences and discipleship.

Predictably, Judy broke up with me for a second time. She apologized for breaking my heart, but the balance in our relationship was seriously off, and it wasn't working. Once she left, I walked, dejected, into the Baja Beach Club restaurant across from the apartment and sat inside a loud, alien-killing video game machine for a good forty-five minutes. Everyone around me seemed to be having a grand time as the summer of 1989 was ending.

"She dumped you?" John quizzed me when I returned from my Baja Beach Club pity party.

I nodded forlornly.

"But wait, didn't you say just the other day that she kissed you?" John's face showed genuine confusion as he continued the post-mortem.

I nodded once more. This time with a grim frown on my face.

"So, let me get this. She kissed you and then she dumped you?" John exclaimed in disbelief.

I sighed. "I don't want to talk about this anymore." And that was the end of it.

John took the hint. "You coming to the I.V. meeting tomorrow? We've got the regional director coming to discuss STIM."

STIM stood for Student Training in Missions and was the InterVarsity equivalent of the Top Gun school. Only mature, godly, and experienced I.V. members were allowed into the STIM program. If selected, they underwent rigorous cross-cultural training in the art of missions, raised their support, and went for short-term mission trips all over the world.

I went to the meeting and listened quietly to the regional director, a Mr. Carl Jenkins, talk about God's heart for missions. His talk was from Romans 10, a book I was now very familiar with.

Casually dressed in jeans and a t-shirt, unshaven, with his well-worn Bible open in his right hand, Carl read with a humble, yet been-there-done-that tone, "And how can they hear without someone to preach? And how can they preach unless they are sent?"

It was at this meeting that things started to change for me as a young Christian. I felt convicted that Jesus had entered my life, but I had not allowed Him to become the center. He was off to one side. Instead, I had allowed a human being—Judy—to serve as the center. And anytime she didn't respond the way I wanted, my whole life was shaken and felt out of control.

I felt burdened as well. Burdened to share this spiritual treasure I had discovered with my friends, extended family, and most importantly, my parents. I needed to go see them. As Mr. Jenkins had said, how else would they hear?

A month later, I was interviewing with InterVarsity about entering STIM several years earlier than was normal for a new believer. I needed training and I think I.V. leadership knew how important this was to me, and that I was headed to Pakistan regardless. So, they accepted my application, with my training to begin in the fall.

STIM was as intense as advertised. While I had much to learn about sensitively sharing the message of Christ with a new culture, or in my case my old culture, the staff was far more focused on us as future missionaries: our insecurities, what holds us back, what motivates us, what stereotypes and biases we hold, and whether we had an accurate view of ourselves and our Creator.

Everything was on the table. We were to forget what we thought we knew about missions, which in my case was very little. But some of the students were missionary kids, or MKs as they were often called, and had a lot more unlearning to do than I.

STIM was a time filled with praying, singing, crying, and releasing things to God that we held dearly. Rooms, closets, or even small cubbyholes of sin kept hidden from Christ—as if we thought He couldn't see them—were exposed. It was painful and then liberating. We all had our own issues and flaws.

I ran into Judy several times that fall. One time, she needed a ride back from visiting a friend, and I was driving back from STIM in my old beat-up Mazda. Over two and half hours, we spoke about what God was teaching each of us. Twice during the ride, my car wound up with a flat tire. I don't remember now how we managed to fix both flats, but I do remember vividly the fun I had even during this small adversity.

Judy noticed my joy and attitude. For the very first time, I had a glimpse of the triangular relationship Christian counselors talk about: you, the girl, and Jesus.

We parted ways with smiles and agreed to stay in touch. No kissing this time.

School, work, and STIM kept me busy as the summer of 1990 approached. To raise the thirty-four hundred dollars I was going to need for my trip, I shared my story with numerous churches. Still, I wondered how I would collect that kind of money.

Clearly, God knew.

Envelopes started to pop up in the mail from all over the state of Texas and even beyond it. Often, the senders would enclose a note: "Ali, we believe God will do amazing things through you. Here's a hundred dollars toward your support. We are praying for you."

No signature. Now that's validation.

One church in Arlington even committed to pay my tuition when I returned. That was huge, because foreign students are required to be enrolled full-time during the semester. To save extra money to buy gifts for my family, I picked up a second job as a waiter at a café in Grapevine. It was there I met Jack Stapleton.

Jack knew the Fox family from his high school days when he and Judy's brother were classmates. As summer approached, Jack and I became fast friends. He came from a broken home and had a tumultuous relationship with his parents.

Jack and I started to speak about God quite a bit. Late one night, he came over. He had many questions about Jesus and wanted to talk. God led me to share with Jack from Josh McDowell's book, *Evidence That Demands a Verdict*. He left around one in the morning, and the next day, I called him in the afternoon and he sounded different—excited.

"Last night I felt like a light transferred from you to me, Ali," Jack said. "I just pulled up at a park near my house and prayed to Jesus."

It was as if God gave me a gift in this exchange, an energy boost to remind me of why I was going to Pakistan, and a reminder of what could happen when we are obedient. I understood that God is the one who changes hearts and minds.

June was fast approaching, and my financial support had miraculously come in. I booked my tickets and planned to stay with a friend in Paris for a week before heading for Karachi. I felt I needed that week alone with God to mentally and emotionally prepare for what was bound to be a difficult trip. Surprisingly, I didn't feel nervous. Instead, I felt strangely focused. In fact, I believe I experienced what many Christians describe as being "in the center of God's will." It was time to go.

June 22nd, 1990, the date of my flight, came soon enough. A shade over four years since setting foot in America, I was heading back to my homeland as a missionary. My checked bag contained Bibles, and I was unsure exactly how I was going to explain that if asked about them as I went through immigration. But rather than worrying about it, I trusted the promise Jesus made in Matthew: "Don't worry what you'll say or how you'll say it. The right words will be there."[47]

As I waited for my flight in DFW's International Departure Lounge, I saw a familiar figure rushing to my gate. It was Judy, looking particularly pretty in a beautiful pink floral dress. Our eyes met.

Our parting was bittersweet, since neither of us knew where this path I was on would lead. We clung to each other until the gate attendant tapped me on the shoulder, saying that I needed to make a choice.

Judy realized she might never see me again after today and whatever label we wanted to put on our cross-cultural romance, it was unique and special. More importantly, she knew that I'd made the greater choice, putting Christ first and *her* second. Painful as it was for her, I believe she liked that order much better.

We both wiped tears from our eyes and waved goodbye. Once again, I was boarding a transcontinental flight, this time heading to my homeland. But now I was traveling for a different purpose. Emotionally exhausted, I dozed off as the plane took off for Paris's Charles de Gaulle International Airport.

I had become fond of America, the land that had offered me the freedom to seek, find, and examine a new truth without hindrance or duress. Such freedom is rare and precious. As I was about to discover, rare and precious should never be confused with safe and secure.

Chapter 8
FREEDOM OF RELIGION PART II: FREEDOM TO BELIEVE

Paris in the summer was as beautiful as advertised. Unlike Dallas, a relatively young city by comparison, this 2000-year-old city with its stunning architecture, gardens, museums, and churches, its cobblestone streets and cafes, was mesmerizing. I was a city boy at heart, after all, and it's hard for a city-lover to find Paris's charm anything less than intoxicating.

The first day or so I simply moped around thinking what a shame it was that I was alone in this city that oozes romance from every pore. Thinking about Judy, I wondered out loud to the Lord, "Will I ever see her again?" The answer was a prompt reminder that I was now married to Him and that I had a purpose for being in Paris before heading to my homeland. That purpose, I believed, was to understand more about the Holy Spirit, the mysterious third person of the Trinity. It was the Holy Spirit whose role, according to the Bible, was to act as my guide, counselor, and coach.

Now that I was learning that converting to Christianity entailed a whole lot more than pats on the back and potluck lunches in affluent North Texas churches, God and I had to have a serious conversation about how I was to handle the realities of being a Muslim convert and facing what was likely to be a hostile environment. And like many other conversations with God that men have had for centuries involving stepping out in faith, the plan was thin on details. It sounded like, "Read the Book of Acts. It has stories about other men who faced dangerous situations in my name. Trust me."

The next day, I went alone to the sprawling palace Chateau de Fontainebleau that dates to the reign of Louis the XIII. The 1500-room Chateau was a sight to behold with all its ornate gardens, sculptures, painted ceilings and chandeliers. But what was even more mesmerizing was the Book of Acts which I read from start to finish while there. As it turns out, the Holy Spirit is the central figure in Acts. The book documents what the disciples did after Jesus departed. This was the true test of fortitude for these men of faith. Would they capitulate in the face of adversity? Or would the church thrive? As I discovered, the church exploded onto the scene.

Reading Acts and spending the week in prayer helped me better acquaint myself with the Holy Spirit. I came to believe that He would indeed be there when I needed encouragement and guidance. This was promised: "I will ask the Father to give you another Helper, to be with you always."[48]

I spent the week rooming with an old family friend of ours named Shahbaz. He was a gruff, thirty-something-year-old nominal Muslim, who sold retail merchandise to make ends meet. God opened a window for me to share my spiritual discoveries with Shahbaz. He listened in stunned silence, a lit cigarette in his hand. And, instead of arguing, he beat the same drum that other relatives had already beaten.

"You best get ready to speak to Aunty about all these damn questions of yours, Ali," he lectured, referring to my mother. "She taught us all about Islam when we were young."

Perhaps Shahbaz wanted me to appreciate how out of place it was for me to question Islam, considering Ammi was the family teacher. I felt a familiar anxiety forming in the pit of my stomach. I thanked him for listening and headed to bed. My flight left for Karachi soon. It was show time.

The next evening, my Air France flight took off for Karachi without incident. From my window seat, I took in the breathtaking sight of the lighted Eiffel Tower in all its latticed glory and the Champs-Elysees, two epic symbols of Paris. It had been a wonderful week, but now I pondered what awaited me. My itinerary called for two months in Pakistan. I was both nervous and excited. I felt close to God.

Soon, though, I was going to need God to put some skin on. I needed a mentor, a friend, and someone to speak to and pray alongside.

I arrived at Karachi's Jinnah International Airport after the nine-hour journey and felt my pulse quicken as I deplaned and walked toward immigration. I had never dreamed that I would feel trepidation going this direction.

How ironic.

I pushed the feelings aside and felt a strange peace.

Jinnah International is not exactly a bastion of organization. Lines formed on an ad-hoc basis. Just as you thought you were getting closer to seeing the immigration officer, some official-looking fellow would cut in line holding passports of some VIP. Then there were what appeared to be able-bodied persons in wheelchairs being pushed by staff, also going straight to the front of the line. There were many men in beards—something I had never paid attention to before.

The mood at the airport was decidedly grim. In the summer of 1990, Benazir Bhutto, the first woman to lead a major Islamic state, was quickly losing her grip on power a mere twenty months into her first-elected term.[49] Accusations of nepotism and corruption surrounded her. Violence in Karachi and the Sind Province was rampant. Just like her father Zulfikar, who was hanged by the government eleven years earlier, controversy followed her, and it was difficult to tell fact from fiction.

Some things in Pakistani politics never change.

In addition to this ongoing political turmoil, another dark cloud hung over the nation and impacted urban cities like Karachi. Backed by the United States, the Afghan *Mujahedeen* had recently caused the Soviet Union to end the decade-long Afghan War, but not before almost three million Afghan refugees fled into Pakistan, bringing with them drugs and a *Kalashnikov* culture.[50] Cheap heroin and weapons were in ample supply, and Karachi had demand for both.

Forty-five minutes later, I passed through immigration without a problem and collected my bags to head toward customs. A customs officer wearing a white uniform waved at me, directing me to open my bags at his station. My heart raced again, thinking about the few Bibles I had packed. "Lord, please give me favor with this man," I whispered.

"What are you studying in the US?" he inquired raising his eyebrows as he noticed the Bibles.

"Religion and faith," I blurted out, surprising even myself with the calmness in my tone and the answer that seemed to come from nowhere.

He pawed here and there in my suitcase for a few more seconds but appeared disinterested with my response. He was after big fish and it was evident from the humble contents of my bag that I wasn't one of them.

"*Jayie aap,*" (Move along), he said in Urdu, waving me off.

Thank you, Jesus!

I exited through the International Arrivals door toward the throng of people awaiting their loved ones. Some held ornate necklaces made of roses, a common way to greet special visitors. Out of the corner of my eye, I caught sight of a familiar face. It was Abboo, but I had to do a double-take. It had been three years since I last saw him, but he looked like a shell of his former self. If I had to guess, he had easily lost fifty pounds. He was only sixty-three but looked seventy-five.

Our eyes met, and no smile greeted me. He slowly waved for me to make my way over to him. Then I saw my mother standing next to him. At only five feet, she had been hidden by the crowd. She did the all-familiar head jiggle and they both started to move toward me. Ammi looked just as I had left her. In fact, she might have put on a few pounds. We exchanged quiet hugs. Abboo held on for a long time but didn't say much. The drive home was equally quiet.

I guess the questions will come later.

The questions began that evening and they came fast and furious. Ammi did most of the talking while my father listened, taking in my responses.

"Are you being pressured by the Americans?"

"Are you being paid?"

"Who is this girl that has brainwashed you?"

"Don't you realize the Bible is corrupt?"

Ammi gave me a reading assignment for the next day: *The Bible, the Quran and Science* by Maurice Bucaille, a French scientist who felt the Quran was far superior to the Bible.

At the onset, I tried to be loving and kind in my responses, but I was finding this inquisition overwhelming. My parents' reactions were the opposite of what I had anticipated. I had expected my mother to be emotional and angry. After all, she was akin to a religious scholar in our family. She was the one who taught me about Islam. And I was expecting my father, the businessman, to be far more logical in his questioning, asking me questions about the veracity of the Bible, the logic of salvation in Christianity, the evidence of the crucifixion, and comparing the Trinity to polytheism.

Instead, what I found was a broken man. A deep sadness had penetrated his heart that was gut-wrenching to behold. He viewed himself as a complete failure as a father, a man, and a Muslim.

Ammi, on the other hand, had a more fatalistic approach to my apostasy.

"*Jay thai na bhala nay matey,*" she quipped with her favorite mantra. "Whatever happens, happens for the best."

She believed that "Prophet Jesus" had reached out to me in America because He was more accessible to me there, and she fully expected Him to lead me straight to the last and final prophet, Mohammed. Shia Muslims believe that all the Prophets from Adam, to Abraham, to Moses, to Jesus were preaching Islam.[51]

The bottom line for her? I was merely confused and there was nothing to worry about. She was going to add this to her prayer list: that Prophet Jesus would lead me to Islam.

I was devastated to learn that both my parents were facing persecution and insults from the entire family. They had failed to raise me to follow the "right path." The fact that I was adopted was cited as a reason, I was told. Town gossips gleefully whispered juicy details about my misdeeds and my parents' equally horrific failure to raise their only son to be a good Shia Muslim.

The fact that my dear parents were being judged and persecuted felt worse than anything anyone could have done to me personally. It was second only to their desperate pleas with me to label my decisions as mere "crimes of passion."

"Just say that you became a Christian because you love this girl," Abboo urged. At times, when there was a "love marriage" in Pakistan where the boy or girl was from a different Muslim sect, one of them would convert to keep the peace and make the marriage more acceptable to the community. Usually the one from the less-religious family would flip.

"I wish I could say that, Abboo," I said, anguished. "But I am not doing this for her." The disappointment on his face was crushing to witness.

Later, Ammi pleaded with me. "My dying wish is that you would come back to Islam." I couldn't do anything but embrace her and weep.

The standard of a collective Islamic society is like-mindedness. Put another way, "If you love me, you must think like me."

It was excruciating, and I was connecting the dots fast. The real issue was not that I was calling myself a Christian or going to a church or reading the Bible.

Those things, while not ideal behavior, could all be tolerated if I attributed them to something, anything, other than actually believing what I was saying.

It hurt immensely to realize that I could cause all this pain to disappear with a few words. But even as a young believer, I somehow knew there would be no turning back once I did.

Hiding in my bathroom and holding on to a tiny green Gideon Bible, I read Jesus' ever-powerful words:

"Therefore whoever confesses me before men, him I will also confess before my Father who is in heaven. But whoever denies me before men, him I will also deny before My Father who is in heaven."[52]

Another realization I came to is how Muslim society measures love. The standard of a collective Islamic society is like-mindedness. Put another way, "If you love me, you must think like me." Pakistani parents couldn't comprehend having a child claim to love them dearly yet not be willing to follow their faith. The two are inextricably bound.

After the first week of this onslaught, I sat outside on the patio that overlooked the night lights of Karachi and wondered whether it would have been less painful for my Muslim parents to do what I had heard some parents do in similar circumstances: hold a funeral, write the apostate out of the will, and kick them out of the family. Or worse.

While I was very thankful that I had not faced physical violence, I was quickly learning that persecution of the emotional kind left painful scars as well.

In the midst of this misery, I received a much-needed shot of joy. Abboo came home the next day from his office with a small stack of letters. "I neglected to give these to you," he said, looking guilty. He held out one envelope. "This one has been here since a day before you arrived."

I recognized Judy's dainty print and took the letters from him, trying hard not to snatch at them. I quickly excused myself and went to my room to read.

Her letter made me smile. It was amazing how written words that had traveled over eight thousand miles across the globe could bridge such an enormous distance. I suddenly felt closer to my Texas home. Judy's letter was full of encouragement, as were the others from members of churches where I had shared my story or from InterVarsity friends. Some were from complete strangers, telling me they were praying for me. I had no idea that these nine letters were to be the first of over 200 I received during my trip. Seven of them would be from Judy. The next morning, I quickly jotted down a note to her and popped it in the mail.

Thus far, my interactions with my extended family members had been less strained than expected. Everyone was practicing a policy of "Don't ask, don't tell," and I was relieved about that. But there were subtle signals everywhere, such as my Uncle Akbar inviting me for "coffee" and then later handing me a book on Islam.

Because I was interested in staying alive, I adopted a quick sounding-board process with the Holy Spirit, whereby I would selectively share as guided by Him, but not compromise my faith. For example, my uncle and father both wanted me to accompany them, per tradition, to the mosque for *Eid* prayers. *Eid ul-Adha* is an annual celebration observed by Muslims worldwide remembering Abraham's willingness to sacrifice his son and God providing a lamb instead.[53] Muslims believe it was Ishmael not Isaac, though, whose life was spared by God.[54]

I reasoned there was nothing wrong with prayer, even if it followed the Muslim prostrating motions, as long as I was praying to Jesus. After all, the twenty-four elders fall prostrate before God and worship Him in the book of Revelation. The Holy Spirit approves this decision within milliseconds and off to the mosque I go with Abboo and Uncle Akbar. Then, in the middle of praying, I am alerted in my spirit to the fact that Shias must bow down and touch their forehead to what they view as a "holy stone." I hear the Spirit say something to the effect of "Mayday! Mayday! Potential idolatry ahead. Bowing to stone is not acceptable." So, I carefully slip the stone aside and continue praying. All is well.

I found these ongoing conversations with God both exhilarating and draining, and I remembered that even Jesus needed a break. Occasionally, he would head to quiet places in the mountains to be refreshed and filled.[55] I was learning the valuable lesson that I was merely a vessel and could not serve God effectively if I was completely drained.

Hours of discussions, buckets of tears, and several weeks later, Ammi decided that it was time to bring in reinforcements. She walked into my room with a bag full of audiotapes and my childhood tape recorder. "I need you to listen to these *majlis* tapes. These sermons, as you all call them in the States, will help you."

Thus began a concentrated effort at deprogramming. *Majlis* are intense sermons given by the Shia Mullahs. I was to listen to the tapes and then share my questions with her. Begrudgingly, I agreed to listen.

The tapes, which were in Urdu, contained sermons on many mystic stories about the prophets and the fundamentals of Shiism. Of particular interest to my mother were the prophecies about the Hidden *Mahdi*, the Twelfth Imam, in whom many Shias believe.

> ***There are ninety-nine names for Allah in the Quran. Not one of them is Father.***

As a descendent of Mohammed, the *Mahdi* was to come at the end of the age to conquer and convert all to the true path of Islam. Shias believe that this promised Messiah will be accompanied by none other than Jesus himself, who will direct the Christians of that time to follow the Mahdi.[56] All would be vanquished who refused to submit to the will of Islam.

To Ammi's dismay, hours of listening to the mullahs drone on did not change my heart. I found the tone haughty and lacking compassion.

Each day that I now saw the religion of my birth up-close, the many rituals and rules, the reading and praying in Arabic without knowing the language, the value placed on external piousness, the more I saw our own feeble efforts to please the Almighty that were devoid of a living breathing relationship with Him. There are ninety-nine names for Allah in the Quran. Not one of them is Father.[57]

Days went by. Conversations became stunted between my parents and me. At night, I overheard hushed discussions and, at times, arguments between my parents in their bedroom. It was as if it was dawning on them that this was more than a nightmare from which they would both wake. It was real. Their son was not some confused teenager who could be verbally slapped into submission.

One evening as we sat down for dinner and I quietly bowed my head to pray over my meal, Abboo blurted out, "We want you to go see Doctor Shirazi for a checkup." Dr. Zubair Shirazi was a family friend and one of Karachi's leading psychiatrists, with degrees from the States.

I let his suggestion sit in the air for a long ten seconds as he gazed at me looking for a reaction.

"Why?" I said, trying hard not to sound defensive as I felt my emotions rise. "Do you think I'm crazy?"

"Just for a few days. Your mother and I need to sort through this," he said, tears welling up in his eyes. "It has all been arranged. You leave tomorrow morning."

Compassion, and not anger, now surged through me. How badly I wanted to see my father saved and to experience God the way I was, for him to know Jesus the way I did.

My mother sat stone-faced, but I could clearly see the look of disappointment on her face. She, our family matriarch, had failed to convince me and now the matter was being escalated to the professionals. The implication in sending me to a psychiatric hospital was clear. Since I wasn't willing to admit that my choices were made under duress, perhaps a diagnosis of mental instability would serve. Frankly, any description would suffice except for the one of which I had become convinced, the one spoken by Jesus himself: "I am the way and the truth and the life. No one comes to the Father except through Me."[58]

The next day I was dropped off at the clinic and spent hours "on the couch" with Dr. Shirazi asking me questions. Looking back, that wasn't altogether a bad thing. I needed to unload on a good listener. I preferred a pastor, but a psychiatrist would have to do.

Shirazi was in his late forties, had a relaxed tone, and was dressed in comfortable-looking khakis and a fashionable blazer. I noticed he was clean shaven. He gave me some tests, but stuck no needles into my brain, thankfully. I shared my story with him as he listened intently and asked many questions, taking notes on his yellow notepad.

Dr. Shirazi turned out to be an Omnist.[59] As far as he was concerned, it was all good: Jesus, Mohammed, Shia, Sunni, Christian, or Muslim. His report to Ammi and Abboo did not encourage them. I was not insane. He believed I would come around once the spiritual high wore off.

I took a rickshaw back to the flat. Upon my return, I found Abboo browsing through some of my Christian books. He was extremely agitated. In an anguished tone he said, "No matter what you do, you will never convert me." He dropped that day's mail on the dining table before me. Another ten letters from believers around the world. Another letter from Judy.

"I am sorry, Abboo, but I find these books helpful," I responded, lowering my voice.

I didn't know how much more emotional torture I could take. The next day Abboo developed a high fever. Ammi called out to me. "This is your doing," she said. "If he dies, it's your fault."

That was it. I had to get out of there. After three enormously long weeks, I could no longer face this alone. I rushed to my room, grabbed my notebook, hid my passport, snatched my father's car keys, and stormed out. I was crying uncontrollably as I drove Abboo's old Mazda through the city. "Jesus help me! This is too much! Too much!" I screamed at the sky.

During the summer, most missionaries travel to the mountains in Pakistan where it is far cooler than humid Karachi. Prior to leaving Texas, I had taken down the names of a few of them but did not expect to find them. As I drove aimlessly through the busy streets of Karachi, I caught a glimpse of a cross on top of an old church and was drawn to it.

Perhaps someone will be there I can speak with.

I parked, wiped my face, walked up to the door, and knocked. As I waited, I noticed that attached to the church was a clinic marked with a Red Cross and posters about drug addiction and its evils.

A Pakistani man opened the door. "Hello," he said. "How may I help you?"

"Uhm, I need to speak with someone. A missionary perhaps." I said. For some strange reason, I felt that I needed to speak with a white western person who was a follower of Jesus. That's all I had known in my short Christian life.

"I am sorry, but Mr. Crenshaw is not scheduled to be back for another week. However, here is his home address for when he returns." He handed me a card.

I looked down at the card with a Red Cross on it. Reverend Elliott Crenshaw, P.E.C.H.S. Society.

That's not that far from where I live, but I don't have a week. I need someone now.

"Is there something *I* can help you with?" the man asked.

"No, thank you," I said, feeling uncomfortable. I didn't know who I could trust at this point. I thanked him and left.

I drove off, dejected, placing Elliott Crenshaw's card in my notebook. Karachi was a city of over fifteen million and it was rush hour. I wanted to get lost amidst the thousands of cars, bikes, buses, and street vendors. It was surreal how alone I felt despite being surrounded by a sea of humanity.

For the next hour, I continued driving aimlessly while speaking with the Lord. What had I gotten myself into? I was only twenty-two years old. The rest of my friends were finishing college degrees, getting married, finding good jobs, and living the good life. Their families were proud of them.

Why me, Lord?

But even as I asked this question, I heard a soft voice speak to my heart: *You did not choose me, but I chose you and appointed you so that you might go and bear fruit.*[60]

I nodded in acknowledgement, and as I did, I looked to my right through the open car window. At that moment a strong breeze opened the page in my notebook where Elliott's card lay, and I noticed the address of the house I was passing. It was the house right next to the one listed on Elliott Crenshaw's card. I slammed on the brakes.

What are the odds of that? What the heck? But lacking a better plan, I decided to stop the car and knock on his door anyway.

Beautifully-kept white rose bushes graced the garden and on the stoop was a welcome mat. Above the door a framed verse from the Bible silently proclaimed: "As for me and my house, we shall serve the Lord."[61]

My pulse quickened. I knocked on the door. Nothing.

Cursing my bad luck, I turned around to head back to the car when I heard something. It was a child's voice. Someone was home. I knocked again, louder this time, and a white man opened the door. He carried a blonde child, a little girl, in his arms. "Hi there, friend. How can I help you?"

"Are you Mr. Crenshaw? Mr. Elliott Crenshaw?" I stammered in disbelief.

"You are looking at him, mate." He smiled. "Come on in and have a cup of chai with me," he said, waving me in. Dressed in native attire, Crenshaw was about six feet tall, had a scruffy blonde beard, curly hair, and glasses. But it was the smile that stood out the most.

As it turned out, Elliott and his wife, Victoria, and their five children had returned earlier that afternoon from Murree, a mountain resort town up north. They cut their plans short because Elliott felt the impulse to get to Karachi a week sooner.

Elliott did a lot of listening that afternoon, and then he prayed for me with a depth I had never experienced. "Come, Holy Spirit, come. Comfort my brother here. He's gone through a lot, Lord. Give him rest."

I felt peace that surpassed understanding washing over me. It was like taking a very long and restful nap. God had put skin on.

Elliott worked with heroin addicts, hundreds of them, in Karachi. I was aghast to hear that one in six males in Karachi was addicted to heroin.[62]

"So, how many doctors do you have in your facility?" I asked, thinking an operation of that size would require a significant team of medical professionals.

"Doctors of medicine or divinity?" Elliott asked, smiling. His response confused me.

"What do you mean?" I said, a quizzical look on my face.

"Just one. Me." Then, he said. "We simply pray for them, Ali. Jesus does the healing. We've seen Him deliver dozens of men out of addiction."

I was intrigued. Elliott and his team formed cell groups who prayed together, ate together, and held Bible studies together.

"Why don't you come on Sunday and join us after church?" Elliott asked.

I immediately agreed.

As Elliott walked me to my car, he looked around to ensure none of his neighbors or their security guards outside the gates were listening. He lowered his voice and said, "Remember Ali, be very careful who you share with about what you have heard. Also, be wise in how you share your faith with relatives and neighbors. This is not Dallas. This is Karachi, Pakistan. There are blasphemy laws."

I nodded, wanting to ask many more questions, especially about the blasphemy laws he'd mentioned, but knew that we would have to find more private time later. I thanked Elliott profusely for his time.

After four wonderful hours spending time with the Crenshaw family, I was off for home. My spirits were lifted and my confidence in God was restored. On the drive home, I praised God for meeting my needs in what I fully believed to be a miraculous answer to prayer.

When I went to the office with my father the very next day, I read an op-ed in Dawn, the national English newspaper of Pakistan, about a Christian woman accused of violating the blasphemy law. The author decried the misuse of this law that was put into place by the former President General Zia-ul-Haq with the support of the Muslim majority parties of Pakistan.

The law allowed for wide latitude for anyone, usually a member of the majority community, to accuse someone of uttering something against the Quran or the

Prophet. Very little evidence was needed with the local police to jail the accused. And the courts, it seemed to me, were obliged to comingle *Sharia* law with traditional jurisprudence when dealing with such matters. And in some cases, especially in rural areas, the issue never made it to court. The tribal or village *jirga* (council) served as judge, jury, and executioner. The penalty could even be death. According to the article, the law had become a convenient vehicle to settle personal vendettas. This made me both sad and concerned as I could see how a simple difference of opinion about faith matters could erupt into a false accusation.

Christ loved not just America, but the world. Believing in Him meant I was now part of a global family of kindred spirits from many colors, languages, and backgrounds.

Pakistan, of course, is not alone in such measures against minorities. Freedom of religion, speech, and the right to a fair trial and defense are rare in the Muslim world.[63] Democracy is a convenient label to secure IMF funds and UN recognition, but in my view, Pakistan still feels like a theocracy at its core. That said, I am glad to note that the recently elected Pakistani Prime minister, Imran Khan, has at least taken a stance against the mistreatment of minorities when found to be falsely accused under the blasphemy law.[64]

In the following days, I saw amazing things. I saw young men miraculously cured of their addictions. I saw men who looked just like me opening Bibles in Urdu to seek God's wisdom. But what I found most remarkable was that they were digging into the same scriptures I had in my English version. I sang songs in Urdu in the cell groups, but the tune was the same as ones I'd heard in America. I prayed with them to Jesus, but in the Urdu language.

It is difficult to explain how transformational this was. It was dawning on me that the truth I had discovered was far from a Western one. Christ loved not just America, but the world. Believing in Him meant I was now part of a global family of kindred spirits from many colors, languages, and backgrounds. This unity I was experiencing with strangers was uncanny and completely transcended culture. There was no denying it.

Weeks went by and I became adept at honoring my parents and family while also honoring God. My parents noticed these changes and their guard dropped just a bit. I started to kiss them goodnight and pray for them aloud in the name of Jesus. On one occasion, when my mother's back was hurting, I asked permission to rub her back and pray for her. She acquiesced.

"I like how you pray to God," she said when I finished.

I was stunned. I grew bolder, sharing creatively with my extended family and friends, but being careful not to disparage their faith. I often thought about Judy and wrote to her regularly. The end of my time in Karachi was approaching.

I had grown by leaps and bounds during my nearly two months in Karachi. God was doing His work here in Pakistan just as He was in the US. I was in awe of His creative genius and how He chose to use people in his plans versus just snapping his fingers to make things happen.

One example of this was when Elliott gave me a book titled, *I Dared to Call Him Father*, by Bilquis Sheikh, a wonderful story of a Pakistani woman who came to know Jesus right about the time I was born, 1967. I was engrossed. Later that week, I visited the home of a very wealthy and religious cousin of mine, Sajida, who had graduated from Duke. As Sajida prepared tea, I browsed through the reading material on the coffee table. To my shock, I saw a copy of the same book lying there.

What in the world? I wondered as I flipped through it.

At that moment, Sajida walked in with an American girl friend of hers. "Jenny is visiting Pakistan from Ashville with her family," Sajida mentioned by way of introduction. "She and her family are here to vaccinate kids up north in the villages. She just gave me that book, so I haven't read it yet," Sajida continued, while mixing the tea with milk and sugar.

It took me two seconds to connect the dots that Jenny and her family were missionaries.

"Actually, I am reading this book, too." I said.

"You *are?*" exclaimed Jenny, startling Sajida a bit.

"Yes, it's a great book so far. Sajida, you should read it, and then I'd love to discuss what you think about it," I gave Jenny a wink and moved on as she gaped.

I was learning that nothing was outside of God's reach, and His creativity in using those willing to submit to His will was limitless. It was also His way of reminding me that He was engaged in what was going on with me. It was inexplicable and otherworldly.

My last Sunday after church, Elliott asked me to join a group of men who were surrounding a fellow named Amjad who was experiencing extreme back pain every time he entered the church. When he stepped out of church, the pain left him. Elliott looked straight at me and said, "Ali, why don't you join these men to lay hands on Amjad to pray for the evil spirit in him to leave?"

"Uh…me?" I gasped, feeling the hair on the back of my neck standing up.

"Yeah, you," said Elliott. "Come on," he gestured.

My heart pounding, I placed my hands on Amjad, along with three other men, and started to pray. As I placed my hand on his shoulder, I felt the fear inside of me dissipate. Words of the Apostle Paul from the book of Romans echoed in my brain: *Nothing can separate you from the love of God.*[65]

I could feel a battle underway inside Amjad's body. He started to shake uncontrollably and foam at the mouth. His pain would subside and then return. This went on for twenty minutes. Finally, his pain left but whatever was inside him remained.

Elliott explained that there are times when such spirits require much confession, prayer, and fasting. But I felt that this situation was as much for my own growth as for Amjad's healing. I needed to understand that I was an enlisted soldier in a spiritual battle. A war was raging all around me, a battle for souls, including those of my parents. Men like Elliott Crenshaw were on the front lines.

During my two months in Pakistan, Elliott introduced me to many fellow soldiers: translators, teachers, prayer warriors, administrators. It took all kinds. Some were American and British people who had given up the comforts of Western civilization to share the good news, but there were also many local Pakistanis. Some were born in Christian homes; others were called out of the Muslim faith, like me. I wondered if God wanted me to become one of these. Was I to come back to Pakistan? I didn't know the answer to that question.

On my last day in Karachi, Elliott, his assistant David, and I went out to a local hole-in-the-wall restaurant and had delicious *chicken karhai* with fresh *naan* (thick tortilla shaped bread made in a clay oven). I had learned so much from Elliott and his cell group. We laughed about how we'd met—the "God-incident" as Elliott called it. We prayed and said our goodbyes.

I felt a fever coming on that night. Abboo lay on his bed, very quiet. I could tell that he was depressed. That was his modus operandi anytime a sad event was approaching. Ammi was already asleep.

I sat next to him and asked for forgiveness for disappointing him. I reaffirmed that my allegiance to Christ only meant that now I loved him even more. "Do you understand that I love you, Abboo?" I asked gently.

He put his hand in mine. That was all that was required.

It was August 20, 1990. My twenty-third birthday. Saddam Hussein and his Iraqi army had just invaded Kuwait, the first strike in what would become the Gulf War. Security was at an all-time high as my flight took off for Paris from Karachi via Dubai. While in transit in Dubai, I got to call Judy for the first time in weeks and hear her voice. I could hear the relief in her voice as she rejoiced at my exit from the Islamic Republic of Pakistan.

"I have a lot to share with you," was all I could muster.

"Can't wait to see you at the airport," she said.

Leaving Paris for Texas on another plane, I continued to make entries in my journal about all that had transpired.

I smiled a tired smile. I wasn't sure if God wanted me to come back and serve alongside Crenshaw or others in the future or not, but for now, Texas felt like home sweet home. For the third time in four years, I was headed back to the Lone Star State.

Chapter 9

FREEDOM TO BUILD

It was September of 1990, nearly two weeks since I returned from my providential trip to Karachi. Everything felt different. As I constantly thought about Elliott and the heroin addicts back in Karachi with their meager supply of resources, the riches all around me felt ostentatious. The "Texas-sized portions" served in restaurants made me think of the beggars everywhere back home.

Why didn't I see these things before?

I wished I could transport my entire church to a developing country for a week. The things they would see, smell, hear, and feel would change them.

On a more positive note, Judy and I had been joined at the hip since I'd returned. Since we wrote to each other so much during my trip, in some small measure she'd experienced what I'd experienced. And showing her all the photographs I'd taken made it even more real. We prayed together for the people in Karachi: for Elliott and his family, for the persecuted Christians in Pakistan and, of course, for my parents. I felt a deeper connection with Judy than we'd ever experienced. I wasn't quite as anxious to impress her. I was simply me: a servant of God first, and all other things later. And just like that, there was balance.

> *I wished I could transport my entire church to a developing country for a week. The things they would see, smell, hear, and feel would change them.*

To celebrate our reunion, I visited a Christian bookstore to purchase a gift for Judy. After walking around looking at various gifts, I selected a wooden music

135

box that played a pretty tune that was only vaguely familiar and had the message, "May the Blessing of the Lord be Upon You."

The checkout man smiled as he wrapped it. "Congratulations, young man." he said.

"Thank you, sir," I said, thinking that was an odd comment for him to make.

But as soon as Judy opened it and heard the tune, she laughed, seeing I was obviously unaware the tune it played was the "Wedding March."

Meanwhile, her mother peeked in from the kitchen with an odd expression on her face. Call it a premonition. The next week, my stomach was filled with gut-wrenching feelings every time I was around Judy. Was God asking me to pop the question?

Where was all this going?

We had broken up three times in three years, yet here we were again and this time everything felt different. My roommate had just gotten engaged and several other InterVarsity friends were also getting married.

I was perplexed, however, by American wedding proposal protocol. My roommate John and his fiancée had already discussed what time of year they wanted their wedding ceremony, where they planned to live after marriage, and the kind of wedding they wanted. This all transpired long before he even bought a ring or proposed. There was zero doubt in his mind what her answer was going to be.

Where is the magic in that?

On the flip side, it certainly seemed less risky. If I ever mustered up the courage to ask Judy to marry me, it would bring our relationship to that proverbial fork in the road, and there would be no turning back after that. So, it was going to be the "Wedding March" or bust.

The next week, I visited my Campus Minister, Mary, to discuss what I was feeling.

She laughed out loud.

"Why are you laughing?" I asked, surprised by her reaction.

"Because it's been a long time since I have met someone in love," she said, this time with a more serious look on her face. "You've got to ask her, Ali, or you'll just make yourself sick."

I desperately wished I could send Mary with my proposal, like the matchmakers in Karachi. So much simpler and safer. Nevertheless, after much prayer and trepidation, I decided this was a risk worth taking. Next to following Christ, it would be the second biggest decision of my life.

Unfortunately, that week I developed a terrible cold. I don't know if it was the cold medicine talking or if I was simply sick of waiting, but I decided to make the forty-five-minute trek to UNT to find Judy. Right there in front of Maple Hall, without the entourage that usually surrounds a Pakistani groom-to-be and without the foreknowledge possessed by the likes of my roommate, ring-less and blowing my nose, I knelt and spit out those fated words, "Judy, will you please be my wife?"

Time stood still. Judy looked extremely distressed. "Uhm, Ali I am so honored by this, but our goals…our goals are so different."

What? Goals? Oh, for heaven's sake.

I promptly got up from my one-knee stance, embarrassed.

"I need time to think," she continued. "Also, you should probably ask my parents' permission."

"Of course. Take all the time you need," I said, not meaning a word of it. I left the campus, dejected.

In Judy's defense, the poor girl had never envisioned a conundrum such as this. She was the "girl next door" who had grown up in a small Texas Hill Country town. She had attended an almost all-white school, made good grades, played soccer at the Y, and attended Indian Princess camp-outs. Apart from dating me, her life had been quite normal up to this point. Even in her wildest dreams, she had never imagined receiving a proposal from a former Muslim from Pakistan. Family factors further compounded her dilemma. She had always imagined a sweet relationship with her future in-laws. That was going to be highly improbable if she married me.

I met with the Foxes the next day. If Judy thought her parents might save her from having to make one of the biggest decisions of her life, it didn't work. They supported me and trusted her. They both acknowledged that they had seen growth in our relationship and in me. Secretly, Jean worried that we would likely starve to death since we were both still students and I was working at McDonald's, but she kindly chose not to verbalize this concern.

Although I don't wish this on any man, the window between the time a man pops the question to the love of his life and the time she says yes or rejects the offer—a rare occurrence in America—is a highly-vulnerable experience. It crystallizes where one's security lies.

You have done all you can. You can't impress her any further. It's verdict time. She must weigh all the factors and decide. Are you the one she can't live without?

My fate was finally decided seven days later. We were sitting in the student union. Judy kept the suspense going for a bit, but I could sense resolve in her mood, and she was smiling. A good sign. Finally, as she was deep in thought, I asked, "So what are you thinking?"

"Oh, I am thinking I would really like to be your wife," she said, smiling cheekily.

And that was that. We made plans to marry the next June, nine months away. We would live in Carrollton between Denton and Arlington. Judy was going to finish school first, and I would complete my final two years at UT Dallas in Richardson, which was nearby.

My parents viewed my engagement as a confirmation that I had lied about my profession of faith not being based on Judy's influence. Letters poured in from my father—twenty-page letters, full of pain and accusations of my having known all along that this was in the future. The letters mercilessly reopened wounds from my recent trip, wounds that were just barely starting to heal. One letter from Abboo said it all. He used to have a poster in his office that had a quote that said, "Peace comes not from the absence of conflict in life but from learning to cope with it." Referencing that quote, he wrote, "Ali, I have no way of coping with such conflict."

We had a beautiful small wedding at the Little Chapel in the Woods on the TWU campus in Denton, Texas. Pastor Tommy Nelson performed the ceremony and several of my family members were present. Sadly, Ammi and Abboo did not attend, but had friends stateside who represented them. To make the marriage acceptable to my Pakistani family, Judy and I agreed to have a *nikah*, a Muslim wedding ceremony. We felt this was acceptable because it was nothing more than saying our vows to each other in Arabic in front of two Muslim witnesses. My cousin Nazneen and her husband served as those witnesses. And just like that, five years after arriving in the USA, I was a married man.

My Western wedding

My Eastern wedding

Here comes the bride

Here comes the *dulhan*

In anticipation of moving to Carrollton and needing to generate more income, Judy encouraged me to consider finding a new job, preferably one that didn't require me to wear polyester pants and come home at two in the morning. Of course, her mother was thrilled with this prospect as well, since supporting us both while making $5.50 per hour didn't seem feasible. It was time to test the transferability of all the skills I had learned in the fast-food business and try my hand at something else.

A week later, an advertisement in North Lake's student job placement office caught my eye: "Customer Service Representatives Needed, Wage: $7.00 per hour." It was with a local consulting firm and the hours were a stable forty hours per week. I applied, interviewed well, and was hired. Little did I know that this event would be the beginning of an entrepreneurial journey that would shape my future.

During the interview process, I learned that this company specialized in helping Fortune 500 employers secure tax incentives. Specifically, what I found most interesting was how this business focused on a nuanced area of the tax law buried deep in the Internal Revenue Code—a jobs credit. This program offered lucrative tax relief to employers who hired the economically disadvantaged. It intrigued me that an entire business could be formulated around a niche piece of legislation.

I quickly picked up the business of tax credits and found it surprising that as an accounting major, I had never heard about these things. Tax credits were like money that helped companies reduce their tax payments to the government. In fact, the more I studied the United States Internal Revenue Code, the more I learned that it had thousands of laws established to encourage, limit, reward or discourage certain economic behavior.

I was awed by the millions of dollars we were capturing for our clients and the success it had brought our company. The parallels between this success story and that of Ray Kroc, my former employer in the fast-food world, were strangely similar. One mastered the art of selling a hamburger served in a fun, fast, and family-friendly environment and then replicated it across the country. Here, a company had figured out how to serve a different product—a tax credit—in a streamlined, customer-friendly and easy way. Just as with the fast-food business, an end-to-end consistent process, automation and excellent customer service were at the heart of it all. It was another American success story, albeit a less public one, and it fascinated me.

I worked full-time, went to school full-time, maintained a 3.8 GPA, and tried to juggle my new role as a husband. Judy graduated and found a part-time job at a fabric store as we struggled to make ends meet and adjust to married life. Judy was adamant that we pay off all my college debt, and we were slowly chipping away at this goal. Having grown up with no training in fiscal stewardship, I was the spender and she was the saver. In premarital counseling, we learned that financial struggles are one of the leading causes of stress in marriage. That couldn't have been truer. I needed to find more income.

> *The ability for the poor, the non-elite, and the minority to have a shot at real success was a true test of whether American democracy and capitalism worked.*

I got my first taste of it in the not-too-distant future. The company offered a contest for the best results for the preceding month. Out of a hundred-plus customer service reps, I was ranked #1 and I received an immediate $1,500 cash bonus. *I could really get used to this pay-for-performance thing.*

As I observed my employer's pattern of success, and as I took more business courses, I couldn't help comparing this and other successes I saw all around me to how things operated in the East. I was amazed by what I was learning in my business law course about American jurisprudence and how it was designed to protect the rights of entrepreneurs. Any person, regardless of age, race, gender or socio-economic background could file for a patent. And, if granted, the US court system was supposed to protect such individuals. Many American companies, such as 3M, amongst others, allowed or even encouraged their employees to innovate while they were being paid.[66]

I found this concept of, "A rising tide should raise all ships," unique and refreshing. I had never heard of this before. In Pakistan, rich feudal lords got richer while suppressing the poor. To me, the ability for the poor, the non-elite, and the minority to have a shot at real success was a true test of whether American democracy and capitalism worked. I was beginning to believe that the American economic system was a true meritocracy. If you had the skills, desire, and willingness to work hard, you had a real opportunity to make a path for yourself.

That is all you can ask for.

And since many of the American CEOs landed in their executive chairs after starting their own businesses or clawing their way up the corporate ranks, they often appreciated that even the entry-level employee deserves the same chance they themselves craved years ago.

The system of business laws and regulation I saw around me in the United States appeared designed to protect against the survival-of-the-fittest mentality that I had witnessed in Pakistan as well as to protect against governmental overreach. For instance, you could work hard to build an empire in Pakistan, and then the government might decide to exercise a nationalization program like it did in the early seventies under Zulfikar Bhutto's reign as prime minister. Major industries from steel or petrochemicals to utilities and major banks were all taken over by the government. This progressivist strategy eventually failed and was reversed.[67]

When such draconian measures go unchecked in a society, it does not leave room for any real incentive for the entrepreneurial spirit to flourish. I saw a lot of wisdom in the body of laws instituted in America to account for such potential tyranny and to guard against the natural human inclinations toward abuse of power and conflicts of interest.

Likewise, I saw laws that attempted to neutralize the disadvantage in America for the under-represented. Businesses were not allowed to give preferential treatment to the white majority when it came to promotions, pay, or government contracts. Rather, there was a set of laws, enforced by agencies such as the Department of Labor and the Equal Employment Opportunity Commission (EEOC) etc., that corrected our natural bent toward bias. In a jungle, the lion does not jump in between the cheetah and the deer to protect the meek. Nature takes its course. Not so in America.

Compare this to places in the Muslim world where certain jobs are relegated to only minorities. Even though the constitutions of countries like Pakistan may prohibit discrimination, the reality is that it is next to impossible for a minority to achieve a high post in business due to their religion. This holds true even to this present day. In 2017 the Asian Human Rights Commission highlighted a grotesque advertisement for sanitary workers posted by the Hyderabad Municipal Corporation. The ad invited applications for the job of sewer cleaner—from non-Muslims only. Applicants were required to take an oath on their religious holy book (e.g. the Bible) that they would never do anything but work as a sanitary worker and would never refuse to carry out the work.[68]

Any man or woman could put their hand to the plow—to grow, seek, build, invent and innovate.

I concluded that America was unique when it came to freedom of entrepreneurship because of its justice system. I loved the symbolism behind the blindfold worn by the lady holding the scales of justice. In many countries in the world, including my country of birth, it is impossible to achieve business success without bribery. They go hand in hand. Yet what good is such ill-gotten success if one must live with the guilt of it?

The laws in America discouraging corruption give entrepreneurs the confidence that their ideas and property will be protected, and their bids to prospects will be judged on merit. Such confidence fuels the entrepreneurial spirit. Any man or woman could put their hand to the plow—to grow, seek, build, invent and innovate. In my view, such freedom was unique. And I could not wait to have my shot at this dimension of the American Dream.

Perhaps it was the immigrant in me that longed to someday own my own business, but as time passed and I learned more about the tax-consulting business I found myself enamored with understanding how the company generated income. As the inbound customer service rep, I was on the front-lines. That is where the value chain began. I befriended every department and asked many questions, trying to discern how other functions fit into the process which ultimately led to invoicing our customers. Although the operation was highly fragmented, I eventually felt I'd figured it out. We were delivering a great value for a fair fee to our clients. Business was booming.

However, although the company was faring quite well, and I was a high-performing employee, there was a pattern of "dangling the carrot" by management that was not setting well with anyone. It seemed that Managers-In-Training remained "in-training" forever. Some managers and employees were labeled as "golden" for a few months and then were ostracized. New products were announced and then disappeared. Bonus programs were announced and then changed without notice.

I won a trip to a "warm climate destination." They sent me to Baltimore—in December! And it was a working trip!

Two years later, I was about to graduate cum laude with a degree in accounting. I wanted to sit for the CPA exam as soon as possible. Many of my classmates were interviewing with local accounting firms to begin the grind of becoming auditors, but as nerdy as this sounds, I was still in love with tax credits.

Graduating from UT Dallas, a seven-year journey finally completed

My moment of decision came when I got sucker-punched by my boss. Twice. (Not literally, mind you.) I had been pining for a managerial position. My boss told me I had the position but asked me to write and post the job description merely as a formality. After all, I had been working in the posted role for four months already. One day, I was called in and told that I wasn't ready for the job. The reason? "You didn't punch in correctly."

Whaaat? You have got to be kidding me. That's the best reason they could come up with?

The second offense felt worse than the first. My supervisor informed me that I was getting a raise. A whole dollar an hour more meant a lot to Judy and me at this stage in our lives as we continued to claw out of my college debt hole. A week later, the raise was withdrawn without explanation.

An employee scorned can be a bad thing. But a highly-inquisitive Pakistani immigrant with an accounting degree and a desperate wife can be a force to be reckoned with. I quickly found another job at a bank in downtown Dallas as a telebanking associate. My customer-service experience coupled with my accounting background made me a shoo-in. But this was only a stop-gap measure while I figured out how to launch my own consulting firm.

In 1993, at the age of twenty-six, I founded REACH Consulting with a buddy of mine from UT. Jason and I had met in my cost-accounting class. We both jumped in headlong, also working other full-time jobs so our wives didn't kill us because of the immediate drop in cash-flow that almost always accompanies such ventures.

During my studies about American history and business, I was always impressed by the way great entrepreneurs ventured off on their own, holding fast to their dreams and ideas, and ultimately prevailed. In hindsight, perhaps due to lack of page space, those history books never did full justice to the trials and tribulations of being a cash-poor sole proprietor with a young wife, debts, and zero credibility.

After three months of knocking on doors of many small pizza franchisees, Jason and I were failing miserably. My old roommate, Assad, was my first and only client. And he didn't want to pay me until he received a benefit back from the government—a six-month-long process. Judy was getting increasingly impatient, wondering when I was going to do what normal CPAs do, a sentiment shared by Jason's wife. REACH was out of business almost before the ink dried on the incorporation papers.

During those days, Judy and I were attending Bent Tree Bible Church, an up-and-coming church in Carrollton. The church was thriving under a young pastor named Pete Briscoe and many families were being added to the church every month. The elder board of the church was also full of bright and seasoned businessmen. One such man was Ron Salmon, who owned and managed a local CPA firm. As an MBB (Muslim Background Believer), I was something of a novelty in the church and, as a result, knew many members. One day, I had the opportunity to share my predicament with Ron. "I am telling you, sir, there are tax credits that can help companies, but for the life of me, I can't sign anyone up."

Ron was in his mid-forties with slicked-back greying hair. He wore crisp, collared shirts and ties, and oozed credibility and integrity. He was also a strong man of faith. "Well," he said, quickly glancing at his leather organizer, "why don't you come on over to my office on Wednesday at, say, three o'clock and we can talk about it. Okay?"

I agreed and thanked him profusely for the opportunity. Wednesday came and I dressed up in my only blue blazer and headed to his firm. It was my first exposure to a genuinely professional environment. Ron had about a dozen CPAs and staff who worked underneath him. His well-dressed secretary showed me to a small conference room.

"Mr. Salmon will be right with you," she said, offering me coffee.

There was a marble-topped table in the conference room. Right there, in the middle of it, was a black, spiral-bound, Research Institute of America (RIA) binder with the Internal Revenue Code opened. Ron's glasses lay on top of the open binder. I could see the words, Jobs Tax Credit, highlighted in the code with notes everywhere. Right then, Ron entered. "This thing is real," he said. "How'd you like to do this for my clients?" And just like that, my intrapreneurship career was launched.

Intraprenuers build businesses inside organizations. Unlike entrepreneurs, they don't go broke quite as easily, but they also don't strike it rich like Steve Jobs or Mark Zuckerberg. The job was going to pay me ten dollars an hour plus a portion of the profits. I was giddy.

"I am so proud of you," squealed Judy as we both celebrated the prospects of having more than spaghetti in our future.

Working for Ron was refreshing. There was so much to learn from him. He was a great coach and teacher. I went to client lunches with him to do "selling" as he called it. The first one was memorable. We met his client at a restaurant. I was armed and ready with my spiral-bound booklet. I noticed that Ron subtly picked it up from the table and placed it under my chair while continuing the conversation with the client.

"Your Orioles were on fire this weekend, Sam," said Ron, making him smile ear to ear. This continued for almost thirty minutes as we ate.

When am I supposed to introduce the topic of tax credits? How long are we going to talk about baseball? Good grief. I thought this was a business lunch.

Still, I sat patiently.

Forty minutes into the hour we had for lunch, Ron made his move. "Ali has some great ideas for you, Sam. It's gonna save you a ton of money. Ali?"

That was my cue and I jumped in to explain with Ron helping translate, at times, when I got too technical. Sam asked a few questions and then ended the lunch with a request for a contract.

Boom! Just like that. We had sold our first project. I resolved to forget about cricket and learn everything I could about baseball, football—both college and pro—basketball, March Madness, and whatever else would help me connect with customers. Much to Judy's dismay, one of the top ten reasons she had cited during premarital counseling for why she chose to marry me—that I didn't care about American sports—was falling apart. That summer, thanks to Ron, I fell in love with relationship selling.

Of course, I not only had to sell the concept, I had to deliver on the promise. Thankfully, my McDonald's training in service combined with the intimate knowledge of the tax credit paid off, and we started getting clients. This was a niche area and I was amazed at how other larger firms, even the "Big 6" accounting firms—Pricewaterhouse, Coopers & Lybrand, Deloitte & Touche, Ernst & Young, KPMG, and Arthur Andersen—did not offer services in this narrow area. In fact, a man at our church who worked for Ernst & Young (EY) referred a few customers to us.

Business was growing rapidly, and I was loving my work-life and moving steadily up the entrepreneurship learning curve. While my fellow UT graduates were stuck in the routine grind of audit or tax work, I was starting to get a small share of the profits. I felt God's hand clearly in these developments.

Later that year, I sat for the Uniform CPA Exam, one of the hardest academic challenges in professional services. In those days, there were four dreadful parts: Audit, Taxation, Business Law, and Financial and Governmental Accounting. I couldn't believe it when Judy called me at work three months later to inform me that we had received the "larger envelope" from the Board of Public Accountancy in the mail. The larger envelope generally meant you had passed. Indeed, I had passed on my first try. Hallelujah! In fact, I had just narrowly exceeded making the "300 club" (all four minimum required scores of seventy-five). I had an eighty-one in Tax.

With genuine excitement on his face, Ron rushed to my cube to congratulate me when he heard the news. As I look back at my business career, I have learned a lot about mentors and sponsors. They are not the same. A mentor is someone who helps coach you and guide you. They give you candid feedback. And they play a critical role in your development. A sponsor is even more. A sponsor may do all the aforementioned, but he or she also takes personal risks on your behalf. They advocate for you at key moments when opportunities arise. They help clear roadblocks. Ron Salmon was my first sponsor. He took a big risk by investing in this new business despite skepticism from his fellow partners. As a good protégé, I delivered, and things were looking up. As I was about to discover, Ron was only the first of several key sponsors God had lined up for my career.

Not everyone was pleased with my newfound success though. That weekend Judy and I visited our old college friends, Rick and Melinda Browne. Rick was also an accountant and had job-hopped quite a bit since graduating. Our wives sent us off to buy ice cream to go with the apple pie Melinda had baked. On the way to the store, I shared with Rick the great news about my passing the CPA exam.

He suddenly grew quiet. Then, to my astonishment, he said, "I hear they have quotas for you guys, don't they?"

Did he just say that? Does he seriously believe the only reason I passed the CPA exam is because I am brown-skinned?

I couldn't believe it. All those horrible feelings of Mr. Pitts from UT Arlington thinking I had plagiarized my paper on "The Sound of Silence" came rushing back.

"No, there is no quota, Rick." I said in a steely tone that caused Rick to drop the topic and switch immediately to ice cream flavors. On the drive back home, I quietly pondered why Ron's perspective was such a polar opposite from Rick's.

Where does this prejudice come from?

I decided that there will always be insecure men in the world, no matter what.

The fall of 1994 brought a season of change. On October 15th, Judy gave birth to our first daughter, Mollie. It was surreal being a young father. Relations with my parents were thawing out a bit and they wanted us all to visit them in Karachi the coming summer. The fall of 1994 also brought me to a fork in the road professionally. The tax law around which I had built a thriving business for

Ron expired. I had a decision before me. I could choose to do the traditional stuff CPAs do—audit, tax return prep, etc., or I could try my hand at tax incentives on a state and local level. However, to do the latter, I would need to find a much bigger firm with larger clients.

"I think you should apply to a Big 6 accounting firm like EY," Ron advised.

"Why? I like working here. What would a Big 6 firm teach me?" I said, somewhat cockily.

"Well, they'd teach you how to walk into a room full of people and act like you know what you are talking about," quipped Ron.

As a former employee of KPMG—one of the big firms—he spoke from experience. I took Ron's advice and wrote a letter to the audit managing partner at EY. Not having a master's in tax, I didn't think I could get into the tax practice. A few days later, I followed up and caught him live on the phone. To my surprise, he immediately encouraged me to apply to their tax practice since, "everything you've been doing is tax credit work."

I changed the name on the letter and fired off a second letter to EY.

A week after Thanksgiving, EY's State & Local Tax (SALT) practice leader for the Dallas office asked me to come in for an interview. I interviewed with five different people at EY over the course of the next few months and ultimately received an offer to start as an Experienced Staff (second year) with the SALT practice. Five years with McDonald's, two years with the tax credits company, six months at the bank, and another eighteen months with Ron, a total of nine years of full-time work experience, translated into a single year at my rank at EY. It is sometimes difficult to assess how prior experience will transfer to a public accounting firm environment, hence, I was initially hired as a second-year staff (Staff 2). But I was simply thankful and hungry to jump in at any level and get started.

Getting into a Big 6 accounting firm as an accounting major the way I did was akin to making a NCAA Division I sports team as a walk-on freshman.

I was raring to go and eager to prove myself. While I emphasized my passion for tax credits, wanting to build a practice, as I had with Ron, my supervisor nudged me toward more traditional income tax work.

"We're not gonna build a tax credits practice, Ali," she flat out told me.

I nodded and got busy prepping state tax returns in the day and studying tax incentives at night. I waited for my break.

My lucky break came soon enough. It was 1996, and Debra von Storch had recently been named the partner-in-charge of the Southwest Region's SALT practice. In Debra I found a kindred spirit and future sponsor. She was gregarious and a bundle of energy; she was also a fierce competitor willing to take calculated risks.

"I have heard about you!" she exclaimed when she stopped by my cube on the fourth floor in San Jacinto Tower in downtown Dallas.

"You have?" I said, glad to hear that a busy partner had some clue about my existence.

"Of course, I have. You are that 'credits guy,' right?"

"Uhm…yes," I said, a smile forming on my face immediately.

"So, why aren't you building a credits practice for us? Let's get started, buddy."

Goodbye reverse triangular merger tax returns, and hello tax credits. Over time, Debra and I became better acquainted. She nicknamed me Prince Ali and with her support, I was busy building one of the first tax incentives businesses in all of professional services as a second-year staff member. The mid-1990s were booming years for most large tax advisory firms like EY. The economy was doing well, and it seemed like everything we touched was growing. I introduced myself to many partners in the Southwest Area, including David Alexander, the area managing partner. What I found refreshing about the EY culture was that rank didn't matter to these partners. They cared about what a person brought to the table.

Every Friday morning at seven, there would be a managing-partner meeting in David's office. In a town-hall meeting held with staff a week earlier, David had casually mentioned that anyone with new business ideas was welcome to drop by. I didn't realize that no one ever responded to those invitations, so I showed up. It was just me, David, and two other managing partners.

With Debra at my manager promotion event

What I will always remember about these meetings is that not a single person looked at me oddly or told me that I didn't belong. They went about their business and listened to my ideas. After several Fridays of me showing up alone, I finally took the hint and stopped attending.

With the support of Debra, David and others, my career took off. They gave me the freedom to build a small business that became a big business inside the multibillion-dollar organization that was Ernst & Young. Leadership also acknowledged that I should have been hired at a higher level. My prior jobs had already trained me well in customer service, in sales, reading profit and loss statements, and in applying tax law to build a business. EY provided me with the perfect environment to apply all of these acquired skills to build new services around tax incentives.

Due to my performance and the revenue that followed, I was fast-tracked from Experienced Staff, to Senior Staff, to Manager, to Senior Manager over the next three years. Twelve years removed from that very first flight to the United States from Pakistan, I was a Senior Manager in EY's prestigious National Tax Department with nationwide responsibilities.

In February of 1997, Judy and I had our second child, a son we named Noah, and moved into our first home in Richardson not that far from my alma mater, UT Dallas. Going from three dollars and thirty-five cents an hour, living in my car at times, and borrowing from friends and relatives to survive, to making six figures was quite the turnaround. I knew the hand of Providence was behind it all. I also knew that this land of opportunity, America, was the good soil that was causing me to bear fruit. But I wanted more. I longed to be a partner.

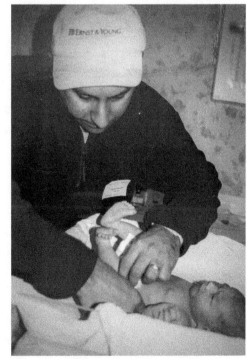

Working dad with baby Noah

As an immigrant, there was something powerful about becoming an equity partner at a firm like EY. Few reached that pinnacle. Fewer still that were of my descent. It symbolized far more than mere financial success. It was acceptance. It was an acknowledgement that I belonged. It was equity of an altogether different kind. If making it into the firm as Staff 2 was like making the cut for a Division I school team, then making partner would be like getting drafted by the pros. I desperately wanted to play the game at the highest level.

In May of 2003—six years and two more kids later— my family and I were enjoying a vacation in Ruidoso, New Mexico when I got a call from yet another sponsor, Gary LeDonne. "Ali, I want to be the first to give you the good news that you have made partner with our firm."

I couldn't believe it. It was really happening. After all the hard work, travel, time away from family, clients, new service ideas, sales, wins, and losses, I had finally achieved the milestone I wanted. Abboo would be so proud, I thought. Every time I had visited Karachi, he had asked me about it.

The phone rang all day that May of 2003 in Ruidoso. Mentors and sponsors somehow found the cabin phone number. It was so very gratifying to hear from them, to hear the joy in their voices. You never, ever make partner on your own in a firm like EY.

The American Dream isn't about what you can ultimately achieve in terms of financial success. It's about your visions and aspirations being within your grasp if you are willing to strive for them.

I could go on to extol the other amazing business experiences I have had since that grand day. But someone much wiser than me said the following about making partner in professional services: "It's like you won a pie-eating contest and they bring you your prize—and it's another pie." That about sums it up—you enjoy the moment and the festivities that follow, and then you get back to the grind.

Twenty-three amazing years have flown by at this firm that I love. It's been thrilling to build many new services alongside my colleagues, to share relationships with the best of the best in corporate America, and to develop other protégés and pay forward the gift of sponsorship. As I look at my entrepreneurial journey, which is far from over, I cannot comprehend any other nation where this would have been possible. Only in America does the "invisible hand" of capitalism[69] and the visible hand of the rule of law co-exist so beautifully. The latter allows the former to flourish. If making more money than I had ever dreamed of, living in a beautiful home, being debt-free, and not having to worry too much about my retirement is the American Dream, then I can yell out, "Bingo!" But I believe the American Dream goes far beyond the material dimension.

The American Dream isn't about what you can ultimately achieve in terms of financial success. It's about your visions and aspirations being within your grasp if you are willing to strive for them. That is all a person can hope for, to be able to pursue happiness. Achievement is never promised in the Bill of Rights. Therefore, equity should never be confused with equality.

Freedom to pursue happiness simply means that the very real barriers that exist in culture and organizations—barriers created by human nature and bias— are removed or at the very least reduced, so one can run his race with an equal chance to cross the finish line based on his skills, talent, and performance. To me, that's what the American Dream is all about. I am truly thankful to the many men and women who helped clear a path for me to run my race.

What about you? Whose path are you clearing?

Chapter 10

FREEDOM TO SELF-GOVERN

November 1993

I sat in our small apartment at our kitchen table, staring at the official-looking white envelope that had just arrived from the US Immigration & Naturalization Service (INS). It had been over two years since Judy and I tied the knot and I had received my temporary Green Card. I knew I had no reason to be nervous as I opened the envelope, but I felt anxious, nevertheless. It was the perpetual state that most non-US citizens lived in—at least those of us from developing countries.

Any contact or interaction with the INS was nerve-wracking. Why? Because they wielded so much power over your future. A simple stroke of a pen and one could be banished to return to the Third World. A family united or not. A chance for continued employment or not. And I was a *legal* immigrant. I cannot imagine how insecure life would be for the many undocumented ones.

The envelope contained what I had hoped for: my pink-colored Green Card. Don't ask me to explain why they call it "green". I was just happy to have this legendary document I had heard so much about. The card gave me the right to live permanently in this land that I loved. I now had the right to work, to travel and freely re-enter the country, to be drafted into the armed forces, and to have the same protections and rights as the citizens of the great State of Texas. I possessed all the rights of citizenship except one: the right to vote.

Eventually, I would have this right as well, once I became a naturalized citizen. Once again, there was a process and a path defined for those who obeyed the laws of the nation. At twenty-six, I didn't fully appreciate the right of self-government and electing leaders. Ironically, all the other freedoms I have extolled thus far would not exist without this fundamental right made available by the US Constitution to her citizens. The power of the ballot held sway in America, enabling the voters to make their voice known every few years. And this was true at all levels of government—state, local, and federal.

Growing up in Pakistan, I did not appreciate the profound wisdom of such a form of government. I never saw Ammi or Abboo vote, nor did I hear much about any of my relatives participating in elections.

The elections were certainly out there. They were often talked about in the papers, but all I recall is the chaos that surrounded them. There were always complaints of election riggings. The feudal lords who owned the lands and hence the lives of thousands of laborers controlled the votes.[70] In Pakistan's 56-year history, the 2013 election was the first time the people of Pakistan experienced a bloodless transfer of power. *The Economist* put it aptly when it said: "…in Pakistan, the bayonet has always trumped the ballot.[71] In Pakistan, a post-election concession speech made by an incumbent is like a unicorn. Once you hold the power in your hand, you rarely give it up willingly, and there are no checks and balances to force you to. Is it any wonder that only the military had the ability to pry open the grip of one tyrannical or corrupt leader after another? But the generals haven't been immune to the lust for power either.[72] Often intervening to remove a bad actor, they can become seduced themselves by the desire to control Pakistan.

As I write this book, the latest drama in Pakistan's depressing history of politics has taken an intriguing turn with the emergence of Imran Khan, our former cricket team captain, being elected the new premier. Of course, keeping up with tradition, this 2018 election has not been without controversy and accusations of election rigging.[73]

I have experienced over thirty years of freedom of government in America, and for me, the profundity lies in the actual execution of self-government: allowing free, fair, and safe elections to transpire; letting the people speak, and, when there is a dispute, having a peaceful process by which to resolve it.

Whether it is the 2000 Bush-Gore presidential election dispute that was resolved by the Supreme Court, a statewide election resolved by a recount, or even a local election settled at a city hall, the American system of government is set up to preserve the integrity of elections. This is a true democracy in action:

where voters, elected officials, judges, the free press, radio talk show hosts, special counsels, and even social media all play their respective roles. Are the results perfect? Far from it. No nation is perfect. But I firmly believe these struggles make us a stronger republic. This may sound a tad naïve, I realize. But this book is about the freedoms I see myself and millions of others enjoying in this nation as compared to what I have witnessed in other countries. As I delved deeper in the tax incentives business as a consultant with EY, I had a front row seat in observing how American government functions at the local, state, and even the federal level. I saw how laws and ordinances were passed and how citizens play a role in influencing those laws.

One event early in my career stands out when I was in my second year at EY. Having the unusual task of developing a new practice at EY had allowed me the privilege of operating at a much higher level than my rank called for. In this case, I was leading the negotiation of a property tax abatement before the city council of a small East Texas town. The client was making a major purchase of new equipment and my task was to convince the council that the investment was worthy of property tax relief.

Dressed in a dark suit, I entered my very first city council meeting. The room was packed. The seven-member council sat perched on elevated seats in a semi-circle. Brass name plates identified the council members. City staff mulled around, speaking to the various council members, showing them papers and whispering last-minute details in their ears. Two uniformed sheriff's deputies guarded each entrance. I noticed a distinct tension in the room. Among the spectators was a group of a dozen or so ladies, all sporting blue buttons that said, "Moms against Bonds." A group of black men and women, looking particularly uneasy, were also present. You could feel the racial tension in the room.

The abatement was the last thing on the agenda, so I concluded there were more significant issues afoot. I tried to pick up on the chatter in the room prior to the start of the meeting. As it turned out, the town had just wrapped up an election. The outgoing mayor was black; the new mayor was white. The brother of the outgoing mayor had organized a protest, accusing the incoming mayor of unfair tactics and racism. There was nothing on the agenda about this matter. I noted that six of the seven members on the council were white with two women. The former mayor, a Mr. Clemmons, remained a member and was the only black person on the council. The featured item on the agenda was a petition to put to a ballot vote a two-million-dollar bond issue to expand the library. However, the women wearing the blue buttons were adamantly against the city taking on any debt. I watched all this pre-meeting action, amazed. Never in a million years had I dreamed a city council meeting could be so rich in drama. I couldn't wait for things to get started.

The meeting opened with the new mayor greeting the citizens and thanking them for coming. The city manager reviewed the agenda before the council. The mayor, a Mr. Todd Klein, then walked us through the process of how we were to interact with the council.

"We're going to have discussion about the bond ballot first. We will then open it up to any residents who want to comment. If you have something to say, please approach the front where the mic is. Share your first and last name and address for the record and then share your comment. I ask that you keep your comments brief to allow us to stay on track with the agenda. Thank you."

Immediately, the meeting went off the rails. The former mayor's younger brother, Mr. Shelby Clemmons, approached the mic.

"Mr. Mayor, I've got something to say."

Before Mayor Klein could say anything, the former mayor, now a council member, piped up. "Now Shelby, you listen to me," he said in a stern yet pleading tone. "I don't want any commotion, you hear?"

"It's okay, Mr. Shelby. You may proceed," Mayor Klein said, raising his hand to calm the older Mr. Clemmons.

Everyone was at the edge of their seats. Shelby Clemmons went on far longer than his allotted few minutes. He argued that his brother had been wrongfully accused of incompetence, resulting in him losing his position as mayor.

Mayor Klein and the other council members listened politely, respectfully disagreeing on occasion as Shelby vented his frustration.

"Thank you, Mr. Clemmons. Your comments are duly noted by the council. Please kindly have a seat," the mayor concluded.

I was stunned by the humility, respect, and dignity shown to Mr. Clemmons during this process. I had never witnessed an ordinary citizen, especially from the minority community, speak this way to city leadership with the police standing right there. That would be unthinkable in Pakistan.

Next up, before the bond issue could be discussed, an elderly black woman slowly made her way to the mike.

"My name is Bernice Johnson, 1503 Bedford Street," she said in a crackling voice.

I noticed a few of the council members trying to contain themselves. One of the women rolled her eyes. Ms. Johnson spoke for several minutes about the same issue, sharing her grave disappointment with city leadership. Again, Mayor Klein thanked her and quickly advanced the agenda to the bond issue. I was dumbfounded by how orderly things were.

How are these citizens allowed to walk off free to their homes after making these statements? What freedom!

The discussion on the bond issue was short. All the council was hoping for was to ask its own citizens whether they wanted to go into debt by two million dollars to expand the library. The manager had presented an independent study done by a local planning firm that showed that the library had too much foot traffic and could not sustain the projected future population growth.

As soon as the discussion was over, two well-dressed, button-wearing ladies who looked like they just stepped out of the TV show *Dallas*, approached the council. I saw knowing smiles exchanged all around the room. The coiffed brunette in her late thirties started first.

"Eileen Showalter, 300 Country Club Drive," she stated with an air of confidence. "Todd," she said, addressing the mayor by his first name, "the ladies here disagree with the survey. We don't need to go further into debt, and we don't need to expand until you all can raise the money in cash." She then proceeded to drill the council on the survey, the highlight of which was when she inquired if pet dogs entering the library counted as foot traffic.

The session ended after Mayor Klein simply pointed out that all they were trying to do today was vote as a council on whether to put this issue on the ballot. And, that the entire town could then decide. The measure passed five to two, with the two council women voting against it.

I was next. I was so mesmerized by the proceedings I didn't hear Mayor Klein ask me to approach the microphone. I wanted to stand up and proclaim at the top of my lungs to the entire audience that if this wasn't government "of the people, by the people, and for the people," then I didn't know what was. I wanted to tell them how unbelievably lucky they were to have this privilege. I didn't feel they comprehended their good fortune.

The abatement discussion and vote lacked the fireworks of the earlier items. It was only to put out a public notice reflecting the city's intention to grant an abatement. The motion passed 5 to 1. Mayor Klein abstained since he happened to work for the company plant. Once again, I was impressed by this open and co-determined process of governing.

Over the years, as I became more experienced in dealing with governments, I found this to be a consistent theme. America was unique and more transparent, by far, than Pakistan. And just as the electoral process has its imperfections, so does our legislative process, particularly at the federal level, as our nation and Washington continue to become more polarized. But I will take gridlock over oligarchy any day.

On the morning of September 11th, 2001, I was driving to work when American Airlines Flight 11 slammed into the North Tower of the World Trade Center. I was listening to my favorite sports talk radio when the news broke about the first plane. The thought of a possible terrorist act had just crossed my mind when the second plane struck the South Tower a mere seventeen minutes later.[74] As if on auto-pilot, I turned my car around and headed home to be with Judy and the kids. Being with family seemed like the only rational thing to do at a time like this.

I found Judy and Mollie, who was almost seven, glued to the TV screen, watching in shock. Noah, 5, and Emma, 1, were too young to comprehend the darkness that had fallen on our nation. A few minutes later, the South Tower collapsed as we gaped in horror. Like most of America, we sat there praying. It took just a few days for the identities of the nineteen terrorists to be revealed. As I feared, they belonged to Muslim majority nations. Although no one could interview these men, all indications were that their savage attacks were a *jihadi* war against America, the Great Satan.

I remember thinking that this was going to be a complete game-changer when it came to the West relating to the Islamic world. How was America going to react? How were brown-skinned people like me, who looked much like Mohammed Atta, the pilot of the first plane, going to be treated?

President Bush soon set the tone by stating that "Islam is Peace."[75] Some would argue he went too far. I believe he did the right thing, handling the situation with poise, recognizing people's natural desire to lash out. He placed American values above scoring political points by respecting the dignity of millions of Muslim US citizens, permanent residents, guests, and allies.

9/11 was a test for many in the American majority community. The fundamental principle of judging people based on their individual actions and not as a collective group was tested and, in this author's view, prevailed.

I believe that most of the Muslim world does not subscribe to the terrorist brand of *jihad*. That said, whether Al Qaeda and its terrorists were following the true teachings of the Quran bears further examination. Was it possible that most of the god-fearing and peaceful Muslims like my parents were following a completely different version of the faith than that of Osama Bin Laden? I found it very difficult to reconcile the two, but that's a topic for another book.

For a few weeks after 9/11, I lived in fear as I heard stories of beatings and harassment of "Middle-Eastern-looking" people in New York City and other places.[76] I chose not to go to the airports and drove to client meetings as far away as San Antonio, a five-hour drive. But considering the magnitude of the tragedy, these incidents of persecution were isolated. Overall, most hurting Americans showed amazing restraint. Eventually, I resolved to trust that Americans were going to hear the words of President Bush: "In our anger and emotion, our fellow Americans must treat each other with respect."[77]

9/11 was a test for many in the American majority community. The fundamental principle of judging people based on their individual actions and not as a collective group was tested and, in this author's view, prevailed.

During a subsequent trip to Karachi the following spring, the reaction from my Pakistani family around these world events and the war that soon followed in Afghanistan was jarring. Abboo flatly refused to acknowledge that the 9/11 attacks had anything to do with Al Qaeda. Furthermore, conspiracy theories that the CIA was behind the attack were circulating everywhere in my home town of Karachi.

I was infuriated. The events of 2001 coupled with my visit to Pakistan evoked other feelings in my heart, feelings of deep patriotism and gratitude for this nation that had given me so much. Until 9/11, I had not seriously considered giving up my Pakistani citizenship. Sure, I wanted to become a naturalized US citizen eventually, but things had changed now. It was time to choose. I wanted to proudly call myself an American. I wanted that one last freedom bestowed *only* on citizens, the freedom of governing oneself.

In August of the following year, sixteen years after setting foot in America for the first time, I raised my right hand and pledged my allegiance to the US flag. And, even though a dual citizenship is not prohibited by the US State Department, I believe the oath of citizenship compels one to choose:

I hereby declare, on oath, that I absolutely and entirely renounce and abjure all allegiance and fidelity to any foreign prince, potentate, state, or sovereignty, of whom or which I have heretofore been a subject or citizen; that I will support and defend the Constitution and laws of the United States of America.[78]

While I will forever love the country of my birthplace, this was the only constitution I felt inclined to defend and the only flag I wanted to bear. Its values were now my values. Its challenges, my challenges.

In November of 2002, we were also blessed with our fourth child, Isaac, completing what we affectionately labeled our six-pack. I noticed that the older I became, the faster the clock ran. With a professional job, family, church, soccer games, ballet and violin recitals, life was zipping along in suburban Dallas.

Two years after gaining my citizenship, I had my first chance to vote in a presidential election: 2004, Bush vs. Kerry. What a thrill to go to my registered precinct and have the sweet elderly volunteers guide me to the voting booth, another great example of how the citizenry can participate in government.

Taking the Oath of Citizenship, August 2002

There was no controversy this go-round, and President Bush was elected to his second term. The allure of grandchildren and my rising EY career both contributed to a thawing of my relationship with Ammi and Abboo, and they visited us on multiple occasions. The East is a prestige-based society where social class matters far more than in the achievement-based Western world in which I lived. However, prestige can be enhanced in Islamic societies through achievement.[79]

My past choices had brought shame and dishonor to my family. In some small measure, becoming a CPA, a partner, a successful businessman with well-behaved children and a creative and devoted wife, began to restore some of that lost prestige in my parents' eyes. Over the years, I would make dozens of trips to my homeland and my relationship with my parents and extended family would continue to grow. It is difficult to continually deny and reject unconditional love and acts of service. I had made the decision to put number five of the Ten Commandments from the Bible fully into practice: "Honor your father and your mother."[80]

The Master family, 2005

Rebuilding the bridge with parents, a 30-year journey

On December 27th, 2007, as I was packing my bags for another international trip to both India and then Pakistan, I received a gruesome reminder of the price of politics in Pakistan. While campaigning for a third term, Benazir Bhutto, the former Prime Minister and the first woman ever to lead a Muslim country, had been assassinated at an election rally.[81] A political enemy weaponized a fifteen-year-old suicide bomber to take her life. As with several others killed before her, the mastermind was never found.

Such is the bloody saga of politics, not just in Pakistan but many other nations. It has been said that, "Power tends to corrupt, and absolute power corrupts absolutely."[82] Truer words were never spoken. Over the years, I have come to appreciate the many facets of the freedom of self-government we enjoy in America. But the willingness of those who hold power to cede that very power to the next freely-elected leader cannot be overstated. This is especially true when talking about the wealthiest and most powerful nation on earth. I will state again, our system of government is not perfect. I believe our republic has its own set of issues. I only extol it in comparison to the plight of citizens elsewhere, particularly those with whom I have interacted from other nations in the Middle East.

In 2010, a few years following the Benazir tragedy, we saw the frustrations of many in the Muslim world boil over into protests and riots. The Arab Spring started in Tunisia and quickly spread to Libya, Egypt, Yemen, Syria and Bahrain; and eventually to other parts of the Islamic world.[83] While some change and attention resulted from these demonstrations, for the most part, the protests were quashed by dictators or power vacuums were filled by others who were as corrupt as their predecessors. Alas, the Arab Spring soon turned into what some have labeled the Arab Winter.[84]

The freedom of self-government, this last of the five American freedoms I experienced, is truly a precious commodity and worthy of cherishing. Yet I believe many will not truly appreciate it unless it is removed. I pray that we never have to experience such a lack of liberty to know what we've lost.

PART IV

The American Dream:

An Ideal Worth Fighting for

Chapter 11

GOOD SOIL: THE ENVIRONMENT OF FREEDOM

"You! Don't touch my food with your hands!" he yelled. The young man's angry words echoed throughout the lobby of McDonald's.

The entire store, packed with crew-people, lunch-rush customers, mothers with children, and more than a dozen Martin High School students, all came to a stunned silence, shocked at his rudeness. It was Monday around noon and I was running the shift in my first week as a manager. I had been so excited about my new role. I was "calling the bin" which meant that my back was to the customers as I communicated with the cooks cooking the burgers and sending them my way to be wrapped.

In the restaurant business, you meet, serve, manage, and report to all kinds of characters, but this was a first for me. I slowly turned around to make eye contact with my accuser. He was a fair-skinned young man sporting tattoos and long blonde hair. His bloodshot eyes glared straight back at me.

I decided to stay calm. My hands were clean. It was company policy to wash hands with hand sanitizer before wrapping food. But, as they had taught me in training, the customer is always right. "Yes sir," was all I could muster as I carefully pulled out two wrapping gloves and continued to wrap the food.

"You got a problem with that?" he snapped.

Is this really happening?

I was a mere twenty-four months removed from living in a bungalow in Pakistan with a chef, two maids, a gardener and a chauffeur. And now this punk was treating me like a leper.

I continued to calmly wrap the food, and said, "No sir, I don't."

169

At this point, I noticed two other customers, also white, one a big burly man in a tank top with some significant tattoos of his own and the other, a gentleman in a suit. Both started cussing the young man out.

"Get your butt out of this store before I break your face!" screamed the larger man. Several customers, including the suited gentleman, were trying to restrain him from laying hands on my offender. He continued, "He is trying to be courteous to you, you moron! You are a disgrace to us all."

Several moms piped in their agreement as well, pulling their kids in close.

The young man didn't even wait for his Big Mac. He was gone.

All I could muster was a smile and a "Thank you." I kept working the bin and we all returned to the organized chaos of the lunch hour.

That moment has stayed with me. It was an American moment, where strangers saw injustice and felt compelled to act, to stand-up to evil. The core American values of fair-play, equality, and doing the right thing, even at some personal risk, bubbled to the surface. I was so proud of my defenders. They reaffirmed my faith in common American decency, something that is never mentioned in Eastern newspapers.

As I look back at my own thirty-two-year American journey, I believe the amazing freedoms I experienced and have shared here are not merely a result of my own talent or perseverance. I firmly believe that the liberties I and others have enjoyed is because America is, as it were, good soil. This country is a soil that, more often than not, allows those willing to work hard, persevere, take risks, and do the right thing, to bear fruit. This has been true since its inception.

It is this powerful environment of freedom, this amazing climate of liberty that one experiences in America, that spurs people on to discover and then pursue their hopes and dreams.

Where does this liberty come from? Undoubtedly the roots of these freedoms can be traced back to America's core documents such as the Declaration of Independence, its balanced structure of government, and the Bill of Rights found in the US Constitution.

But many other nations have been founded after achieving independence. What is unique about America? I believe the secret lies in America's core values and their primary source: the Judeo-Christian God. The Founding Fathers' steadfast belief that "All men are created equal" and have been granted "unalienable rights" by their Creator rather than by a governing body, serves as a catalyst for these precious freedoms.[85]

In his best-selling book, *America the Beautiful*, Dr. Ben Carson discusses the supernatural wisdom behind the three-pronged structure of the US government—judicial, legislative, executive—and the checks and balances it avails.[86]

Addressing the probable source of our governmental structure, Carson elaborates:

> Why three branches? The idea was birthed by the writings of Baron Charles Montesquieu, French social and legal philosopher, scholar and writer. Montesquieu wrote the highly influential book *The Spirit of Laws*. This book greatly impacted the formation of the American government, as it was read and studied intently in America... [he] was the most frequently quoted source, next to the Bible.[87] In it, Montesquieu acknowledges the deceit and wickedness of the human heart, as shown in Jeremiah 17:9, and advocates for a system that tries to check and moderate mankind's worse excesses by dividing power into three parts. His inspiration came from Isaiah 33:22, which states, 'For the Lord is our judge, the Lord is our lawgiver, the Lord is our king.[88]

Carson shares many stories about key founding fathers, highlighting their faith and arguing against the belief held by some historians that our Founders were predominantly deist, believing in God merely as a "First Cause" who holds no interest in the ongoing day-to-day events of human life.

Some of the most interesting quotes in the book are from George Washington. In one such quote from his letter to the General Assembly of Presbyterian Churches, Washington states: " I reiterate the professions of my dependence upon Heaven as the source of all public and private blessings...."[89]

In another fascinating account from July 9, 1755, during the French and Indian War, Washington miraculously escapes death and is quoted in a letter to his brother, John A. Washington: "But by the all-powerful dispensations of Providence, I have been protected beyond all human probability or expectations; for I had four bullets through my coat, and two horses shot under me, yet escaped unhurt, although death was leveling my companions on every side."[90] Our first president was a man of faith who believed in a God who was engaged in the lives of men.

It does not take a brilliant prosecutor to prove beyond a reasonable doubt that many of the framers of the original government felt accountable to a higher authority when they devised the rules of governance for our republic. God was acknowledged, beseeched even, and His words used as guideposts throughout the amazing process of ridding ourselves of British tyranny and forming a nation the likes of which the world had not seen before.

> *It does not take a brilliant prosecutor to prove beyond a reasonable doubt that many of the framers of the original government felt accountable to a higher authority when they devised the rules of governance for our republic.*

Nevertheless, it is not my intent in these final chapters to argue whether the original formation of our government was exclusively Christian. Opposing views exist and many books have been written on this topic. My views are informed by my own pragmatic life experience of having lived in and under multiple cultures and governments, having travelled to sixteen countries while closely observing and practicing two vastly different global faiths.

When I contrast the laws and governing principles found in the USA to other nations combined with my own life-experiences, I see the stamp of the Judeo-Christian God all over them.

In an article published by the Heritage Foundation, Mark David Hall, Herbert Hoover Distinguished Professor of Political Science at George Fox University, captures the essence of my point. He contends that answering this question of a Christian Founding with a vehement "Absolutely!" or "Of course not!" oversimplifies things. Instead, he goes on to make a compelling case that Christianity had a strong influence in the principles, documents, and thinking of the Founders.

He states,

> I believe that this is the most reasonable way to approach the question: 'Did America have a Christian Founding?' In doing so, it is important to note that nominal Christians might be influenced by Christian ideas, just as it is possible for an orthodox Christian to be influenced by non-Christian ideas. I believe that an excellent case can be made that Christianity had a profound influence on the Founders.[91]

I have also observed interesting parallels between the structure of American government, which is subservient to its citizens, and the Christian faith. The government is set up to serve and protect the people's rights, not to lord it over them. That seems reminiscent of the words of Jesus: "The Son of Man did not come to be served, but to serve, and to give his life as a ransom for many."[92]

Finally, because these Judeo-Christian values arguably serve as vital underpinnings for the founding principles upon which America stands, I believe it is extremely difficult, if not impossible, to transplant American democracy into countries that do not share such values. Unless a nation's values are inextricably linked to biblical values, a nation doesn't achieve true democracy, because if the people don't believe that liberties come from their Divine Maker, then freedoms are offered selectively, based on man-made criteria. And off we go down the slippery slope.

Humans see worth in the external: riches, beauty, strength, accomplishment, race, religion, sect, or gender. In the biblical story of Samuel, when God is leading him to identify Israel's future king, God says to Samuel about David's good-looking older brother: "Do not look at his appearance or at his physical stature, because I have refused him. For the Lord does not see as man sees; for man looks at the outward appearance, but the Lord looks at the heart."[93]

> *Because these Judeo-Christian values arguably serve as vital underpinnings for the founding principles upon which America stands, I believe it is extremely difficult, if not impossible, to transplant American democracy into countries that do not share such values.*

People in many parts of the world claim to live in a free society. But do they really? How is freedom measured? In the world I came from, there is very little liberty and justice for all. Liberty and justice exist for the rich, the powerful, the elite. But in America, we at least aspire and often succeed to make it available for all.

I realize that not everyone will share this sentiment with me. My book is only an exercise in the relative comparison of liberties I have experienced and then a hypothesis as to their source. Said another way, I am grading America on a bell-curve. There is no such thing as a perfect nation. We are certainly not immune from the dark shadow of injustice that can and does rear its ugly head from time to time here at home. However, I consider America's great aspiration to make liberty and justice available to *all* to be like natural good soil, soil that gets richer over time as old matter dies. It is never fully perfect, but ever-evolving toward that lofty goal aspired by the Founding Fathers. And that's what makes America special.

Chapter 12

GOOD SEED: THE DNA REQUIRED TO FLOURISH IN THE FREE ENVIRONMENT

*A*ugust 22, 1990 – Houston Intercontinental Airport

It was another humid August evening in Houston, and I was about to catch the final leg of my arduous journey from Karachi to Dallas. It had been a life-changing summer. I spent two incredible months sharing my newfound faith with my Muslim family and friends back home in Pakistan. It was, without a doubt, the hardest thing I had ever experienced in my young life. Despite the anguish I faced during this trip, I was amazed at the sweetness of my walk with Jesus. The Holy Spirit, whom Jesus promised, was real and we communicated regularly.

I didn't hear an audible voice from heaven. Often it was through prayer, scripture reading, or the sense of a soft voice speaking to my own conscience. The more I spent time with Him, and the more I obeyed and acted on His prompting, the easier it was to hear. I also believed that suffering for Jesus had something to do with the audio quality—the signal got stronger with pain. Don't get me wrong. I didn't always get excited when I heard God's voice. Often, I responded like Jonah the prophet, who, when asked by God to warn the people of Nineveh of impending judgment, did a complete one-eighty and headed the other way until God thwarted his plans.[94]

I had been traveling since the night of August 20th, Pakistan time—almost 60 hours—and I was exhausted. My flight boarded in ten minutes, and the only thing keeping me placing one foot in front of the other was that I was going to see Judy in less than two hours. In preparation for this occasion, I had found a restroom at the airport, shaved, put on my nice tan khakis and a red-striped button-down that Judy liked. For good measure, I splashed on half a liter of cheap cologne.

As I approached my gate, I overheard a heated argument between the airline gate agent and a young man.

"C'mon, man! I had no idea about these rules," he said, sounding exasperated.

He was about six feet tall, black, and obviously worked out. He wore bright pink baggy Bahama shorts and a yellow tank-top with OP written on it. He completed his ensemble with high-top sneakers.

The gate agent was a tall, middle-aged lady whose blonde hair was pulled back in a ponytail. Her blue uniform was clean and pressed, and she had a distinct don't-mess-with-me air about her. She looked at him and responded somewhat curtly, "I am sorry, sir, but it's airline policy. All dependents of employees that want to travel for free must follow the attire protocol. No shorts and tank tops are allowed. Long pants, shirts and dress shoes only."

"This is bull-crap. I've got to be in Dallas for a photo shoot," he said, pointing to the camera in his hands. By now, other passengers were starting to take notice. Five minutes to boarding.

The attendant was determined to move on and started to ignore him and focus on other passengers needing assistance.

Suddenly, I felt the dreaded nudging from the Holy Spirit and we had a ten-second argument of our own.

You want me to do what? Nooo! Lord, I am tired. This is crazy. Look at him. He is huge. It won't work.

I lost the argument and rushed to approach the young man. Boarding had now started. "What shoe size do you wear?" I asked, hardly believing the words were coming out of my mouth.

"Now, what?" he responded with a puzzled look on his face. And then suddenly it clicked for him.

"Ten and a half," he said with an incredulous look.

"Great, I wear tens. Let's go." I pointed toward the men's room about thirty yards away, and we both sprinted toward it.

The next thing I knew, we were both laughing and throwing clothes over the stall walls. Out he came, barely fitting in my khakis and button-down shirt. It was going to work.

"The name's Calvin," he said, beaming ear to ear and shaking my hand vigorously.

He ran out quickly and I followed, looking utterly ridiculous in his baggy Bahama shorts, oversized sneakers, and the OP tank-top.

Oh boy, Judy's gonna love this look. Thanks, Lord.

They were announcing my name with just minutes before closing the gate. As I was boarding, I enjoyed the hilarious moment, watching the look of utter disbelief on the gate agent's face as Calvin presented himself to collect his boarding pass just in the nick of time.

I believe the willingness to give up our freedom to serve others is a key criterion for success in America.

The only person more stunned than the gate agent was Judy when, dressed in baggy shorts, I introduced her to my new friend. We laughed, exchanged clothes and information, and then said our goodbyes. I never heard from Calvin Stokes after that day. But I am willing to bet he will remember the day a stranger traded clothes with him at the airport.

When nudging me into action, God brought a verse to my mind from the Apostle Paul's letter to the Corinthian Church. "I am a free man, nobody's slave; but I make myself everybody's slave in order to win as many people as possible."[95]

This noble notion of being free to give up my freedom had been impressed on my heart throughout my trip. It's what Jesus modeled. It's how He wanted me to live. Unfortunately, this is not how I live all the time. He simply caught me in an "in-tune" moment.

Why do I tell this story? I believe the willingness to give up our freedom to serve others is a key criterion for success in America. I am not speaking of material success. Financial success sometimes follows; other times it does not. Rather, I am speaking of building a legacy.

If America, with all its empowering freedoms, is good soil, what kind of good seed will flourish in this liberty-rich environment? Not every seed planted in fertile soil winds up bearing good fruit.

As I have observed, those who embody the American Dream begin with courage and the willingness to do what it takes to preserve freedom, not only on our own soil but also beyond it.

One of the most sobering sights in this nation is the Korean War Memorial in Washington D.C. I didn't know much about the Korean War until I visited the site several years back. I remember being astonished by the sheer number of American lives lost in this "Forgotten War," as some call it.[96] Almost 37,000 American soldiers paid the ultimate price, in addition to over 100,000 who were wounded in combat.

I read two inspiring inscriptions at the memorial. The first was the famous line, "Freedom is not Free." The second, by the Pool of Remembrance, read: "Our nation honors her sons and daughters who answered the call to defend a country they never knew and a people they never met."

More powerful words would be difficult to find. The willingness to give up our own freedoms to preserve the freedoms of others is good seed. Time and again throughout modern history, American men and women have put on their uniforms to go meet evil at its doorstep, to help an ally and keep tyranny at bay from our own shores. But courage comes in many forms, and not only in wearing a uniform and serving your country. It is the courageous person who thrives, grows, and bears fruit in a free environment.

The fruits of freedom are not harvested without risk. Which is riskier, to accept an arranged marriage or to seek your one true love, knowing you risk rejection? Is it riskier to hold on to a status-quo job you don't enjoy or start your own business, knowing more than fifty percent fail?[97] Is it safer to blindly follow your parents' faith or walk into a new place of worship where that faith may be challenged? Risk and the American Dream go hand in hand.

I firmly believe that to thrive and bear fruit in the good soil of America, the good seed must possess DNA that is willing and able to deal with great adversity. As I review the path of my own life, many events appear almost like connecting dots that providentially prepared me for the American soil in which I would be planted years later. Being an only child, neglected, and left unprotected from predators, I formed a survivor's instinct and mentality at an early age. I was forced to be an individual in a highly collective society. To survive, I had to build a toughness to withstand my challenging environment.

Risk and the American Dream go hand in hand.

The American settlers who followed their dream to claim homesteads in the west had to be physically rugged to endure the harsh external elements. Likewise, I had to develop thick skin as a rugged individual to bear things that attacked my internal spirit: persecution, taunting, being treated like an object, being discriminated against.

Put another way, I believe the precarious nature of my early childhood and adolescence may have led to the development of a high Adversity Quotient (AQ), a term coined by Paul Stoltz in his book *Adversity Quotient: Turning Obstacles into Opportunities*.[98] I believe this preordained resiliency allowed me to often take the path less trodden, whether faith, career, relationships and so on. I take no credit for this "high-AQ" DNA. Many immigrants develop it to survive. We are the "tempest-tost" as Emma Lazarus the poet called us.

I believe my adoption was another connecting dot in the picture of my life journey. My birth dad, Imran, did not have the means to send me to the States. He was a car mechanic and made an ordinary living. Abboo and Ammi at least had the resources to send me to America.

Several other dots connected as I discovered the identity of my birth parents. Learning about this sixteen-year-old family secret in the manner that I did had a profound effect on me, and I believe God used it to draw me further to Him. My brain had already withstood the shock of discovering something I believed all my life was not true. Unbeknownst to me, an alternate reality had existed all this time. Perhaps as a result, my brain and heart were more receptive to believing in the full identity and work of Christ. Having my biological identity hidden from me all those years may have enabled me to remain open to the possibility of my spiritual identity also being hidden. That discovery prevented me from simply tossing the Bible into the trashcan from the get-go.

When I learned that God adopted me as His child, I did not reject it immediately because I had an appreciation for the principle of adoption, a concept that is not found anywhere in Islam, where adoption is more akin to guardianship of an orphan but not the carrying on of a family name.[99] Thankfully, Ammi and Abboo chose to go farther than what Islamic law allowed and truly adopted me. Another dot connected, and a full picture began to form, one that showed me that my Creator had a plan tailor-made for me. A coincidence? I think not.

What about you? As you've read about my journey, do you see your own connecting dots? Are they starting to form a picture? Did you miss them? I believe they are there for all of us. Keep looking.

The five freedoms we have discussed herein are precious: the freedom to fail, love, seek truth (religion), build (entrepreneurship), and self-govern (government). However, those who make the most of them and achieve their American Dream, are the ones who are willing to pursue that dream with unabashed passion, perseverance, hard work, and individual responsibility. They don't wait around for the government to lend a hand. Instead, appreciating the good soil in which they find themselves, they seize the opportunity, not only for themselves but also their families and their communities. They become true Americans, respecting and celebrating its traditions and values.

Chapter 13
A CALL TO SAFEGUARD THE DREAM

"Posterity: you will never know how much it has cost my generation to preserve your freedom. I hope you will make good use of it."[100]
John Quincy Adams

August 21, 1990 – Paris

The door to my small hotel room flung open, hitting the metal door stop with a loud clang. A police officer flicked on the room's bright fluorescent light and looked at me as I winced and rubbed my eyes in shock. Then as quickly as he had barged in, he left and slammed the door without so much as an apology.

I glanced at the clock. It was 3:00 a.m.

I couldn't believe what had transpired over the past eighteen hours. A group of fellow Pakistanis and I boarded a flight from Karachi to Paris's Charles De Gaulle Airport. In addition to me, there were three other couples and five children ranging from newborn to twelve. We were supposed to catch a flight from Paris to Houston, but our flight from Karachi was late and we arrived in France just as our Houston connection was taking off.

Missed international connections are never simple problems to solve. Most travelers purchase tickets through discount travel agents offering special deals on air fares, and finding the next available flight can be extremely stressful. This experience is exacerbated when traveling with young children. For my part, I was running a 101° fever much of the flight and was loaded up on medication. Still, my fellow passengers and I assumed that since we had no control over the delay, the French officials would help us find available options.

181

As we deplaned, we noticed an unusually high number of armed guards, trained dogs, and other security personnel seemingly on high alert. The first Gulf War had broken out two weeks earlier, and Operation Desert Shield was well underway.

Several airport officials and two grim-looking armed guards escorted us to the immigration area where we were handed over to a tall French officer who clearly was in charge of the matter. He addressed us first in French, but none of us understood him. One of the Pakistani men who held a Canadian passport tried to convey this to him. "Sorry, sir," he said with a thick accent. "No French."

"Passports. I need your passports, please," the officer responded curtly.

Anytime an official demands a passport from an immigrant who is traveling, the immigrant becomes nervous. Why? Because the passport bears the precious visa stamps allowing you to reach your destination. A lost passport can mean a lost future to an immigrant traveling to the West. Therefore, you never allow yourself to be separated from your passport when traveling internationally. It is a cardinal rule. So, you can imagine how we felt when the tall officer gathered all our passports and walked off with no explanation.

Three long, nervous hours passed without any word. It was now about noon. Children were getting hungry and all the snacks were gone. We had been placed in a small transit lounge that was barricaded with ropes and a guard was posted at the exit. No other passengers were allowed in this area. When one of the ladies with the newborn approached the guard to ask for water, he simply gestured toward the bathroom.

At this point, the Canadian Pakistani man made a run for the exit. Before the surprised guard could stop him, he jumped over the small barricade and made a beeline for the ticket counter across from the lounge. He shouted at the supervisor behind the counter. "We are being treated like animals! We've got women and hungry children!"

Good for him. I took another aspirin and tried to sleep on the lounge chairs, thinking this all felt like a bad dream.

The valiant efforts of our brave Canadian friend helped. An hour and a half later, we were ushered to the ticket counter, and the tall *gendarme* returned with our passports in hand. The Canadian tried to rail on but was interrupted immediately by the officer.

"Gentlemen, shut-up!" he said in a raised voice.

I couldn't believe my ears. *What have we done?* It was now 2:00 p.m. Five plus hours without food or water.

The officer explained that we would be fed soon, and they had booked us on a flight for the following morning. But he added that we would need to be kept under supervision since we had no French visas.

Food was finally served at 3:00 p.m. Wine was offered with lunch, which, of course, the Muslim families ignored.

We ate in silence, feeling utterly humiliated, but as it turned out, the worst was yet to come. After lunch they loaded us into a van and drove us to a nearby motel. It was nearly 6:00 p.m. and I was ready to enjoy some time away from crying children, sobbing wives, angry husbands, and somber security guards. The day's events had thoroughly disoriented everyone.

"Kids will need to go in separate rooms, please," said one of the officers. "Also, men and women will be separate."

Are you kidding me? Will this never end?

Thankfully, the officers allowed the baby to stay with his mother but escorted the young children to a separate room as they cried out, "Mummy!" or "Abboo!" The wives wisely urged their husbands to remain calm, lest they be arrested. I was led to a separate room and instructed to keep my door unlocked.

After undergoing some scrutiny by the US airline security personnel the following morning, we boarded a flight to Houston. The ordeal was finally over.

This short but ugly vignette of my life from many years ago reminds me what we, as Americans and in our various micro-cultures, must continually strive to do. We must be vigilant to stand against racial bias that is motivated by fear and can curtail our freedoms and deny basic human dignity.

Could our experience at Charles De Gaulle ever happen on US soil? Although we would all like to respond with a vehement "Absolutely not!" we would be remiss if we didn't take stock of our own present-day challenges. Not everyone feels free or safe in America today. Negative incidents involving race relations occur with alarming regularity, especially incidents between law enforcement and members of the black community.

I don't want America to become like other nations, allowing fear to drive our decisions. Fear breeds hate. After 9/11, we saw some signs of that, but for the most part we have steered clear of rashly judging an entire people based on their religion, skin color, or nationality. I don't mean to gloss over the blemishes of internment camps from World War II or the sad legacy of slavery. I am saddened to read about these events. I am relieved to read about American presidents stepping up to the plate to offer redress and seek forgiveness and acknowledge the wrong done.[101] In school textbooks, I see future generations learning about the errors of their forefathers. It isn't whitewashed away. That's the only silver lining. I see a nation capable of conceding and learning from its transgressions.

Once again, I want to acknowledge that my current experience as a well-assimilated, successful, Pakistani male married to a Caucasian woman can hardly compare to that of a Muslim woman who observes the *hijab* or a black teen from the inner city.

That said, I believe that America as a nation still grasps the most important point about liberty: that freedom arbitrarily restricted anywhere for anyone will eventually come back to hurt us and our own freedoms as well. Those who have been recently allowing racial fear to get the best of them would be well-advised to remember this.

What of travel bans, refugee caravans, DACA, and the border wall?[102] These are extremely complex issues and, even as an immigrant, I don't profess to have the answers. I want other immigrants to experience the amazing freedoms I have enjoyed. However, I believe we enjoy freedom in America because we are a nation of laws.

While I believe we could and should be regarded as a nation of immigrants—remember the early settlers who took many grave risks to come to this country—it does not mean that the rights of American citizens should become subservient to those of immigrants, whether legal or undocumented.

The Declaration of Independence states: "Governments are instituted amongst Men, deriving their just powers from the consent of the governed."[103] Hence, I believe our government must prioritize the rights of citizens, secure our borders, and continue to provide for legal means to gain citizenship. I hope our leaders can strike the right balance and continue to allow immigrants from all backgrounds who uphold the law and American values to become legally naturalized. Additionally, there must be room for dignity, pragmatism, and grace in this process. Having once faced an unknown future as a young foreign student in this country, I sympathize with the children of undocumented immigrants (aka Dreamers) in the dilemma they face and urge our leaders in Congress and the Administration to work out a compassionate solution.

A "melting pot" is supposed to do just that—melt the various cultures and qualities into a new entrée. But for soup to taste delicious, the ingredients must blend and play their role.

My heart also goes out to the many seeking asylum out of true desperation. Americans are a compassionate people. We can do more. However, striking a compassionate balance where immigration is concerned is far easier said than done. Being a Good Samaritan is not a risk-free proposition. No artificial intelligence can perfectly read minds and intentions. Nor can any vetting process plan for all contingencies and prevent immigrants from turning on their host. I see some coming into this land who want to enjoy America's freedoms but do not respect its traditions. They do not want to assimilate into the culture in a positive way, and their agenda at times is in direct conflict with the core values of their host nation.

I have no great solution to offer other than to keep believing that the same goodness of the American way that grabbed my heart will positively impact the behavior of other immigrants, propelling them to engage and improve not only their own circumstances, but those of their entire neighborhoods and the community at large.

I am not speaking of losing ethnicity. I believe it is possible to retain much of one's heritage and bring it into the host nation in an authentic and accretive manner. I love teaching my American-born friends about the game of cricket and introducing them to my favorite dish of *chicken tikka masala*. A "melting pot" is supposed to do just that—melt the various cultures and qualities into a new entrée. But for soup to taste delicious, the ingredients must blend and play their role.[104]

I entered America as an alien over thirty years ago and have now lived more than half my life in this great nation. Having experienced other cultures, governments, and political systems, it is easy for me to appreciate the superior quality of life and incomparable hope found in America. I once heard General Colin Powell speak at an EY tax conference in Orlando, and he told a story that captures this hope. He shared about taking a walk in Manhattan on Park Avenue on one of the numbered streets to get a New York City hot dog.

"I love the green and red relish they put on those things," he quipped. "You can only find that in New York."

General Powell was our sixty-fifth secretary of state at this stage in his illustrious public service career. He stopped at a hot dog stand which, like almost every other hot dog stand in New York City, was owned and operated by an immigrant. He asked the owner for his favorite hot dog, with the "red and green relish and mustard."

As the Secretary continued, I wondered where his story was going.

"At this point, the man started to pay attention to me and the Secret Service guys and he immediately freaked out, swearing he had a green card," Secretary Powell said.

All 2,500 consultants in the audience broke out in laughter as we imagined this scene unfolding on New York's Park Avenue.

It's no coincidence that freedom and bravery are coupled together in our national anthem. We are free because we are brave.

Powell plowed on with a big grin on his face. "It's okay. It's okay," he said. "Just here for a hot dog."

When Secretary Powell tried to pay for his hot dog, the immigrant man refused saying, "No. No. America has already paid for it." He went on to thank the Secretary for all that America had done for him and his family.

I saw many a Kleenex being pulled out as Colin Powell wrapped up this short but powerful story of why he still felt optimistic about the promise of America.

As I think about the immigrants we want to welcome to our shores, I think of this story and the humility and dignity it represents. If you are a recent immigrant to this nation, I challenge you to fully engage in the American experiment. It's a worthy exercise. I hope reading about my own immigrant journey will inspire you to take advantage of the many freedoms we have discussed here. But remember to enjoy them with an attitude of gratitude.

For those born in America, I say to you, never forget what an amazing country you have. There is none other like it. However, you cannot take these precious freedoms for granted. You must seize the American Dream for your-selves, your children, and their children. You must understand its roots. Too many in our society and leadership are apologizing for America. We are far from perfect, and sometimes an apology is appropriate, but we must refrain from emulating other cultures and systems. There is a reason for the long lines outside American consulates around the world—we are *still* viewed as the land of opportunity.

Have you ever wondered why we are called the "land of the free and the home of the brave?"[105] It's no coincidence that freedom and bravery are coupled together in our national anthem. We are free because we are brave. What does bravery look like for you? What risks will you take to preserve our freedoms? This preservation happens not only on battlefields but in the daily acts of courage each of us must display in our respective spheres of influence.

Perhaps you have been considering becoming a volunteer firefighter or police officer. It could be you have been thinking of teaching in a school in an underpriv-ileged neighborhood. Or maybe you have contemplated serving in your place of worship or running for city council. It's time for action. Your community needs you.

Courage for you might mean speaking up when you see something unethical happening at work. Or as a business leader, instead of going to the same trusted employee you always use, it might mean giving a career-enhancing assignment to a minority employee who—other than the color of her skin—has all the nec-essary qualifications.

Perhaps courage for you would be hosting an international student whose language you do not speak. Many international students spend years in the USA and never see the inside of an American home.

Courage might involve confronting a relative who uses racial slurs when speaking about his Hispanic lawn workers.

It could be any number of these uncomfortable and risky moves. You must decide what bravery looks like for you. But decide you must. Our mutual free-dom depends on the collective acts of day-to-day heroism by people like you and me.

I would like to end with one final experience that captures my immigrant American journey. It involves yet another airport and an airliner. If you haven't caught on by now, strange things happen to me at airports. I suppose when you have almost four million air miles accumulated, as I do, you tend to rack up a few interesting tales.

> **You must decide what bravery looks like for you. But decide you must. Our mutual freedom depends on the collective acts of day-to-day heroism by people like you and me.**

It was the summer of 2000, and I was rushing to the Long Beach Airport to catch a flight home to Dallas for my daughter's ballet recital. My client meeting had run late, and I would be cutting it excruciatingly close, but there weren't many flight options available. Compared to LAX, the Long Beach Airport was diminutive but also easy to get in and out of. That's what I was counting on.

I checked in my rental car and was running full bore to get through security and to my departure gate. I approached just as the gate agent was shutting the exit door that led to the tarmac. I was a full five minutes past my departure time. I made a feeble attempt at begging to board the plane, but she shook her head and gave me a you-know-better-than-that look. I was an elite frequent flyer, but nobody gets on a plane five minutes after departure time and once the gate is closed.

Shoulders slumped, I made my way to the little restaurant upstairs to wait for another five hours for the next flight to Dallas. I was going to miss the recital. I sat down at a table by the window and noticed that a Super 80 jet was still standing on the tarmac. It looked to be at the same spot where I thought my missed Dallas plane was.

Why is the plane still here?

Five minutes passed, and the plane hadn't budged.

Hmm...is there a mechanical delay? Hallelujah! Maybe I still have a chance.

I was an optimist at heart, so I ran back down with my bags in tow to the same gate agent.

"Is my plane still out there?" I asked her, earnestly trying to give her my sweetest I-fly-a-ton-and-am-an-important-business-executive smile.

"No, that is not *your* plane," she responded in a matter-of-fact tone. "That plane's headed to Tampa."

The gate area was virtually empty.

Suddenly she seemed to have a change of heart and said, "Let me see your boarding pass," with a sense of urgency that confused me a bit.

Why does she care? I am here for five hours now.

The next thing I knew, she was talking on her walkie-talkie to someone. Then she looked at me and inquired with a stern voice, "You've got your bags with you?"

I nodded.

"C'mon then. Follow me quickly, please."

I obeyed. The plane was less than a hundred yards away on the tarmac with one of those moving stair-case contraptions being driven toward it.

Naww!

The gate agent looked straight at me, trying to suppress a grin. "This will never happen again. Here you go," she held out a new boarding pass with a smile.

I couldn't believe it, and I was utterly confused.

As if reading my mind, she added, "They will explain it to you when you get on board." Then, she turned and headed back to the gate.

I climbed the staircase, bracing myself for the angry glares of all the passengers, glares reserved for late-arriving frequent flyers who pull their weight to get on a plane at the last second. As the door to the Super-80 opened, I flipped over my green boarding pass expecting to be in the middle seat in the very back of the plane. To my astonishment, the pass read, "6A First Class."

What in the world? I'm upgraded? Cool!

As I entered the plane, I noticed there were no other passengers in first class. Three flight attendants stood there greeting me. "Welcome, Mr. Master. How are you?" a blonde-haired, thirty-something flight attendant asked. Now I noticed that not only was the first-class cabin empty, but so was the entire coach cabin. I had never seen an outbound jet completely absent of passengers. It was surreal.

"Where…where is everyone else?" I asked.

A male flight attendant responded, grinning ear to ear, "You are it, Mr. Master. This is actually a dead-head flight to Tampa via Dallas. You owe a huge thank you to Charlene, your gate agent, and Captain Shelton. Now buckle up, please."

As I followed instructions, I couldn't help smiling.

This is gonna make for a fun story.

After a smooth take off, all three flight attendants were fawning all over me. "Would you care for another meal, Mr. Master?"

"Yes, please."

"More Chardonnay, Mr. Master?"

"Absolutely."

Craig, the male flight attendant, had a Frisbee on the plane and wanted to see if he could throw it to me in coach. You'd be amazed how large an empty Super 80 jet can feel.

Mid-flight, the pilot decided to get in on the fun. His voice resounded over the PA. "Ali, this is Captain Shelton speaking, I hope you are enjoying your journey with us. We are flying over Albuquerque right now heading south toward Texas."

It is hard to match the experience of hearing a voice over a PA calling you by name at thirty-five thousand feet as you gaze into the clouds.

When we landed in Dallas, I thanked Captain Shelton and his crew profusely, and then strutted down the jet-bridge and out the other side. I got a few strange looks from the waiting passengers at DFW when no one else emerged from the plane. I smiled and headed home to my daughter's ballet performance. I was going to be on time after all.

What lay beyond the golden door for me was beyond my wildest imaginations. It was abundant life, liberty, and the pursuit of happiness, and not just in an earthly sense.

In so many ways, what was gifted to me that day in Long Beach, California, is exactly what has been given to me by America and by God. In this country, I have experienced undeserved opportunity and grace beyond measure.

As I reflect on the international flight that brought me to the United States for the first time all those years ago, the words inscribed on the Statue of Liberty certainly have held true for this immigrant. I was indeed tired, poor and without a home. Although I didn't know any better back then, I was yearning to breathe free. I had yet to taste true freedom. What lay beyond the golden door for me was beyond my wildest imaginations. It was abundant life, liberty, and the pursuit of happiness, and not just in an earthly sense.

That is why I wrote this book. I felt Americans needed a fresh reminder of the amazing nation they have and the power of the liberties I see so often being taken for granted. Sadly, in my three decades here, I have witnessed a decline in the very values that make America a great and free nation. Lady Liberty's torch still burns, but her light has dimmed. Few in America appreciate the powerful slogan, "Freedom isn't free." Fewer still comprehend the full impact of those freedoms, having never lived without them.

The freedoms I have highlighted here through my personal journey are just a taste of the many rights bestowed upon us as citizens. I focused on the five that I found the most compelling as I compared them to my life in the Muslim world and they are worth summarizing once more:

- In the *Freedom to Fail*, America showed me that everyone deserves a second chance. The American system anticipates failure on the road to success and allows room for it.

- In the *Freedom to Love*, America offered a culture that allows for a choice to seek out the one you want to spend the rest of your life with.

- In the *Freedom of Religion*, America gave me the gift of discovering and then believing new truth without the threat of persecution.

- In the *Freedom to Build*, America showed me that all who wish to try their hand at free enterprise may do so as hard-working entrepreneurs.

- And finally, in the *Freedom to Self-Govern*, America gave me the privilege to play my part as the governed and to elect my leaders.

If any part of my journey inspires you to safeguard the freedoms we cherish in America, no matter how small or great the measure, then I consider this endeavor a success.

ABOUT THE AUTHOR

Ali Master's perspective on the American Dream is unique. He has personally experienced the freedoms he touts in this book. Because he is a former Muslim, some of these, such as the freedom of religion, came at a great personal risk. Ali is a highly successful managing partner with the global firm of Ernst & Young (EY) and has built and led multiple large businesses. He is a licensed CPA and holds an undergraduate degree in accounting. He is also a graduate of leadership programs from both the Kellogg School of Management and Harvard University. Ali has served as a member of EY's Diversity & Inclusiveness Council and is a frequent speaker on a range of topics from business, to inclusion, to leadership, to Islam. His bi-cultural background uniquely qualifies him to contrast American freedoms and values to those found in Muslim countries. He lives in Texas with his wife and 4 children but travels frequently across the U.S. and internationally.

Follow and Connect with Ali

Continue the conversation around the American Dream, liberties, faith, culture, inclusion, and entrepreneurship by directly connecting with Ali through his site or by following him on his author page on Facebook.

www.alimaster.com

Facebook.com/AuthorAliMaster

To have Ali speak to your organization or group,

please email: alimasterauthor@gmail.com

ℰNDNOTES

Acknowledgements & Introduction

1 Gary Chapman, The Five Love Languages, (Chicago: Northfield Publishing, 1992).

2 John McCain and Mark Slater, Faith of My Fathers, (New York: Random House, 1999).

3 Emma Lazarus, "The New Colossus by Emma Lazarus," Poetry Foundation, Poetry Foundation, Accessed January 11, 2019, https://www.poetryfoundation.org/poems/46550/the-new-colossus.

Chapter 1

4 Sushant Singh, "India-Pakistan 1971 War: 13 Days That Shook the Subcontinent," The Indian Express, The Indian Express, December 16, 2016. https://indianexpress.com/article/explained/india-pakistan-1971-war-bangladesh-indira-gandhi-4429236.

5 "Shah Jahan Biography - Life History, Reign, Administration, Architecture, Facts," n.d. Biography - Life History, Facts, Achievements & Death. Accessed January 11, 2019, https://www.culturalindia.net/indian-history/shah-jahan.html.

6 Barney Henderson, 2017, "Indian Independence Day: Everything You Need to Know about Partition between India and Pakistan 70 Years On," The Telegraph, Telegraph Media Group, August 15, 2017, https://www.telegraph.co.uk/news/2017/08/15/indian-independence-day-everything-need-know-partition-india/.

7 Quora, 2016, "Why Are Dogs Considered Unclean and Cats Clean in Islam?" https://www.quora.com/Why-are-dogs-considered-unclean-and-cats-clean-in-Islam.

8   Peter Niesewand, 2016, "Pakistan's Zulfikar Ali Bhutto Executed: Archive, 5 April 1979," The Guardian, Guardian News and Media, April 5, 2016, https://www. theguardian.com/world/2016/apr/05/pakistan-zulfikar-ali-bhutto-executed-1979.

Chapter 2

9   Nadeem F. Paracha, 2014, "Uprisings and Downfalls: Attempts at Ousting Pakistani Governments," DAWN.COM, October 30, 2014, https://www.dawn. com/news/1141343.

10   History.com, Editors, 2009, "Statue of Liberty," History.com, A&E Television Networks, December 2, 2009, https://www.history.com/topics/landmarks/statue-of-liberty.

Chapter 3

11   Johnny Colla and Huey Lewis, "The Heart of Rock and Roll," 1983, WB Music Corp., Huey Lewis Music and Cause & Effect Music.

Chapter 4

12   "Civil Rights Act of 1964 (U.S. National Park Service)," n.d., National Parks Service, U.S. Department of the Interior, Accessed January 11, 2019, https://www. nps.gov/articles/civil-rights-act.htm.

Chapter 5

13   Nichola Khan, Mohajir Militancy in Pakistan, (New York: Routledge, 2010).

14   "11 Surprising Facts About Fatal Attraction," 2017, Mental Floss, Mental Floss, September 18, 2017, http://mentalfloss.com/article/73920/11-surprising-facts-about-fatal-attraction.

15   K M Hedayat, P Shooshtarizadeh, and M Raza. 2006, "Therapeutic Abortion in Islam: Contemporary Views of Muslim Shiite Scholars and Effect of Recent Iranian Legislation," Journal of Medical Ethics, US National Library of Medicine, National Institutes of Health, November 2006, https://www.ncbi.nlm.nih.gov/pmc/articles/PMC2563289/.

16   "Religions - Islam: Abortion," 2009, BBC, BBC, September 7, 2009, http://www. bbc.co.uk/religion/religions/islam/islamethics/abortion_1.shtml.

17 Jamal, Umair, 2017, "Zia-Ul-Haq and the 'Islamization' of Pakistan's Public Universities," The Diplomat, The Diplomat, March 28, 2017, https://thediplomat.com/2017/03/zia-ul-haq-and-the-islamization-of-pakistans-public-universities.

18 Debra Jacobs, Garrett Sheridan & Juan Pablo González, Shockproof, (Hoboken, NJ: John Wiley & Sons, 2011), 167.

19 "6 Lessons from the 'Founder' of McDonald's," 2017, YourStory.com, Yourstory, February 21, 2017, https://yourstory.com/mystory/3c67120cab-6-lessons-from-the-founder-of-mcdonald-s.

20 Jentezen Franklin, The Fearless Life, (Lake Mary, FL: Charisma House, 2014), 28.

Chapter 6

21 "Islam and Homosexuality: What Does the Koran Say?" Haaretz.com, Haaretz Com, May 18, 2018, https://www.haaretz.com/middle-east-news/islam-and-homosexuality-what-does-the-koran-say-1.5395747.

22 Elaine Sciolino, Special to The New York Times, 1988, "ZIA OF PAKISTAN KILLED AS BLAST DOWNS PLANE; U.S. ENVOY, 28 OTHERS DIE," The New York Times, The New York Times, August 18, 1988, https://www.nytimes.com/1988/08/18/world/zia-of-pakistan-killed-as-blast-downs-plane-us-envoy-28-others-die.html.

23 "Supreme Court Legalises 'Free-Will' Marriages," 2016, IRIN, January 7, 2016, http://www.irinnews.org/news/2003/12/30/supreme-court-legalises-free-will-marriages.

24 "Social Customs: 'Nearly Half of Pakistani Women Are Married before the Age of 18'," 2013, The Express Tribune. The Express Tribune, August 31, 2013, https://tribune.com.pk/story/597697/social-customs-nearly-half-of-pakistani-women-are-married-before-the-age-of-18/.

25 "Religions - Islam: Five Pillars of Islam," 2009, BBC, BBC, September 8, 2009, http://www.bbc.co.uk/religion/religions/islam/practices/fivepillars.shtml.

26 "What Does It Mean to Be Unequally Yoked?" GotQuestions.org, January 9, 2019, https://www.gotquestions.org/unequally-yoked.html.

Chapter 7

27 Avinash Bhunjun, 2018, "What Does Muharram Mean and How Does the Islamic Calendar Work?" Metro, Metro.co.uk, February 1, 2018, https://metro.

co.uk/2017/09/21/what-does-muharram-mean-and-how-does-the-islamic-calendar-work-6944367.

28 Quora, 2018, "Where Did Islam Come From?" https://www.quora.com/When-did-Islam-start.

29 Neil R. Lightfoot, How We Got the Bible, (Grand Rapids, MI: Baker Books, 1963).

30 Matthew 16:15-16.

31 Seyyed Hossein Nasr, and Asma Afsaruddin, 2019, "'Alī," Encyclopædia Britannica, Encyclopædia Britannica, Inc., January 1, 2019. https://www.britannica.com/biography/Ali-Muslim-caliph.

32 "Muhammad: Legacy of a Prophet," PBS, Public Broadcasting Service, Accessed January 12, 2019, https://www.pbs.org/muhammad/ma_quran.shtml.

33 Matthew 5:3.

34 Sadeq Saba, 2008, "Visiting Iran's Ayatollahs at Qom," BBC News, BBC, June 17, 2008, http://news.bbc.co.uk/2/hi/middle_east/7458709.stm.

35 Matthew 5:6.

36 Matthew 5:7.

37 Luke 19:10.

38 Isaiah 53:1-12.

39 Dianne E. Butts, 1970, "Jesus Predicted His Own Death Three Times," Bible Prophecies Fulfilled, https://bibleprophesiesfulfilled.blogspot.com/2014/03/jesus-predicted-his-own-death-three.html.

40 Matthew 20:28.

41 John 15:4-5.

42 2 Corinthians 5:17 (CEV).

43 Mark 3:21.

44 Mark 3:33-35.

45 Matthew 10:22.

46 Matthew 10:24-25a.

47 Matthew 10:19 (MSG).

Chapter 8

48 John 14:16 (ISV).

49 Barbara Crossette, 1990, "Bhutto Is Dismissed in Pakistan After 20 Months," The New York Times, The New York Times, August 7, 1990. http://www.nytimes.

com/1990/08/07/world/bhutto-is-dismissed-in-pakistan-after-20-months. html?pagewanted=all.

50   Falak Sher Khan, n.d., "Impact of Afghan War on Pakistan," LinkedIn. Accessed January 12, 2019, https://www.linkedin.com/pulse/impact-afghan-war-pakistan-falak-sher-khan.

51   "Al-Qur'an Al-Kareem," n.d. Al-Qur'an Al-Kareem. Accessed January 12, 2019. https://quran.com/3/19-20.

52   Matthew 10:32-33 (NKJV)

53   Sanchita Chowdhury, 2018, "The Story of Eid-Al-Adha Or Bakrid," Boldsky, Boldsky, August 20, 2018, https://www.boldsky.com/yoga-spirituality/faith-mysticism/2013/the-story-of-bakrid-035802.html.

54   Jason Jackson, n.d., "Ishmael or Isaac? The Koran or the Bible?" Christian Courier, Accessed January 12, 2019, https://www.christiancourier.com/articles/1161-ishmael-or-isaac-the-koran-or-the-bible.

55   Matthew 14:23.

56   "Special Specifications of Imam Al-Mahdi (as)456," 2013, Al-Islam.org, November 12, 2013, https://www.al-islam.org/shiite-encyclopedia-ahlul-bayt-dilp-team/special-specifications-imam-al-mahdi.

57   Silas, n.d., Wine in Islam, Accessed January 12, 2019, http://www.answering-islam. org/Silas/no_father.htm.

58   John 14:6.

59   An omnist is someone who believes in all religions. "Omnist," n.d., Merriam-Webster, Merriam-Webster, Accessed January 12, 2019, https://www.merriam-webster.com/dictionary/omnist.

60   John 15:16.

61   Joshua 24:15.

62   Nadeem F. Paracha, 2016, "Karachi: What's in a Picture?" DAWN.COM, July 29, 2016, https://www.dawn.com/news/1273993.

63   Angelina E. Theodorou, 2016, "Which Countries Still Outlaw Apostasy and Blasphemy?" Pew Research Center, Pew Research Center, July 29, 2016. http://www.pewresearch.org/fact-tank/2016/07/29/which-countries-still-outlaw-apostasy-and-blasphemy/.

64 Editors, Dawn.com, 2018, "'Do Not Clash with the State': PM Khan Issues Stern Warning to Agitators after Aasia Bibi Verdict," DAWN.COM, November 6, 2018, https://www.dawn.com/news/1442630.

65 Romans 8:38-39.

Chapter 9

66 Charles Coy, n.d., "Reward Failures to Crush Employees' Fear of Innovation," ReWork: Today's Technology Impacts Tomorrow's Talent, Accessed January 12, 2019, https://www.cornerstoneondemand.com/rework/reward-failures-crush-employees-fear-innovation.

67 "Nationalization under Bhutto," 2012, History Pak, March 21, 2012, http://historypak.com/nationalization-under-bhutto.

68 Spencer, Robert, 2017, "Pakistan: Ad for Sewer Workers 'Only for Non-Muslims,'" Jihad Watch, July 15, 2017, https://www.jihadwatch.org/2017/07/pakistan-ad-for-sewer-workers-only-for-non-muslims.

69 "Invisible Hand – What Is Invisible Hand? Invisible Hand Meaning, Invisible Hand Definition," n.d., The Economic Times, Economic Times, Accessed January 12, 2019, https://economictimes.indiatimes.com/definition/invisible-hand.

Chapter 10

70 Saher Baloch, 2013, "Feudal Lords Are Blocking Land Reforms," DAWN.COM, November 7, 2013, https://www.dawn.com/news/1054603.

71 "A First," 2013, The Economist, The Economist Newspaper, March 18, 2013. https://www.economist.com/blogs/banyan/2013/03/democracy-pakistan.

72 "'Military Coups in Pakistan' on Revolvy.com," n.d., Trivia Quizzes, Accessed January 12, 2019, https://www.revolvy.com/page/Military-coups-in-Pakistan.

73 Press Trust of India, 2018, "Imran Khan's Swearing-In In Jeopardy As Poll Panel Withholds Notification," NDTV.com, NDTV, August 7, 2018. https://www.ndtv.com/world-news/pakistan-elections-imran-khans-swearing-in-in-jeopardy-as-pakistan-election-commission-withholds-not-1896874.

74 "9/11 Interactive Timelines," n.d., 9/11 Memorial Timeline, Accessed January 12, 2019, https://timeline.911memorial.org/#Timeline/2.

75   "'Islam is Peace' Says President," National Archives and Records Administration, National Archives and Records Administration, Accessed January 12, 2019, https://georgewbush-whitehouse.archives.gov/news/releases/2001/09/20010917-11.html.

76   Tamar Lewin, 2001, "Sikh Owner Of Gas Station Is Fatally Shot In Rampage," The New York Times, The New York Times, September 17, 2001. https://www.nytimes.com/2001/09/17/us/sikh-owner-of-gas-station-is-fatally-shot-in-rampage.html.

77   "'Islam is Peace' Says President," National Archives and Records Administration, National Archives and Records Administration, Accessed January 12, 2019, https://georgewbush-whitehouse.archives.gov/news/releases/2001/09/20010917-11.html.

78   "Naturalization Oath of Allegiance to the United States of America," n.d., 23.11 Cuban Adjustment Act Cases, | USCIS, Accessed January 12, 2019, https://www.uscis.gov/us-citizenship/naturalization-test/naturalization-oath-allegiance-united-states-america.

79   Christine A. Mallouhi, Miniskirts, Mothers, & Muslims (Grand Rapids, MI: Monarch Books, 2004), 24.

80   Exodus 20:12.

81   Ziad Zafar, 2018, "Who Killed Benazir Bhutto?" DAWN.COM, December 28, 2018, https://www.dawn.com/news/1378568.

82   "A Quote by John Emerich Edward Dalberg-Acton," n.d., Goodreads, Goodreads, Accessed January 12, 2019, https://www.goodreads.com/quotes/749222-power-corrupts-and-absolute-power-corrupts-absolutely.

83   Editors, Encyclopaedia Britannica. 2015. "Arab Spring." Encyclopædia Britannica. Encyclopædia Britannica, inc. January 14, 2015. https://www.britannica.com/event/Arab-Spring.

84   Phil Karber, Fear and Faith in Paradise, (Lanham, MD: Roman & Littlefield Publishers, Inc., 2012).

Chapter 11

85   "Preamble to the U.S. Declaration of Independence, 1776," n.d., Preamble to U.S. Declaration of Independence, Accessed January 12, 2019, https://www.elcivics.com/us_declaration_preamble.html.

86   Ben Carson, M.D., America the Beautiful (Grand Rapids, MI: Zondervan, 2012) 37.

87 William J. Federer, America's God and Country: Encyclopedia of Quotations (St. Louis: Amerisearch, 2000), 453, Quoted in Ben Carson, M.D., America the Beautiful (Grand Rapids, MI: Zondervan, 2012)

88 Ibid.

89 George Washington, n.d., "Quotes of George Washington," Accessed January 12, 2019, http://www.sonofthesouth.net/revolutionary-war/general/george-washington-quotes.htm.

90 John White, 2016, "The Hand of God and George Washington," George Washington Inn, April 15, 2016, https://georgewashingtoninn.com/the-hand-of-god-and-george-washington.

91 Mark David Hall, n.d, "Did America Have a Christian Founding?" The Heritage Foundation, Accessed January 12, 2019, https://www.heritage.org/political-process/report/did-america-have-christian-founding.

92 Matthew 20:28.

93 1 Samuel 16:7 (NKJV).

Chapter 12

94 Wayne Jackson, n.d., "10 Great Lessons from the Book of Jonah," Christian Courier, Accessed January 12, 2019. https://www.christiancourier.com/articles/66-10-great-lessons-from-the-book-of-jonah.

95 I Corinthians 9:19 (GNT).

96 Liam Stack, 2018, "Korean War, a Forgotten Conflict That Shaped the Modern World," The New York Times, The New York Times, January 1, 2018, https://www.nytimes.com/2018/01/01/world/asia/korean-war-history.html.

97 Investopedia Staff, 2018, "Top 6 Reasons New Businesses Fail," Investopedia, Investopedia, July 9, 2018, https://www.investopedia.com/slide-show/top-6-reasons-new-businesses-fail.

98 Paul G. Stolz, Ph.D., Adversity Quotient, (New York: John Wiley & Sons, Inc., 1997).

99 Quora, 2014, "What does Islam say about adoption?" https://www.quora.com/What-does-Islam-say-about-adoption.

Chapter 13

100 Letter from John Adams to Abigail Adams, 26 April 1777 [electronic edition]. Adams Family Papers: An Electronic Archive. Massachusetts Historical Society. http://www.masshist.org/digitaladams/

101 "Japanese-American Internment and Redress: Petition and Coalition Building," n.d., Historical Society of Pennsylvania, Accessed January 12, 2019. https://hsp. org/education/unit-plans/japanese-american-internment/japanese-american-internment-and-redress-petition-and-coalition-building.

102 Hasan Dudar, 2018, "Americans Divided on Whether Immigrant Caravan Is Threat to USA," USA Today, Gannett Satellite Information Network, November 19, 2018, https://www.usatoday.com/story/news/2018/11/19/migrant-caravan-donald-trump-border-security-immigration-poll-threat-central-america-honduras/2055361002.

103 "The Declaration of Independence: Full Text," n.d., Ushistory.org, Independence Hall Association, Accessed January 12, 2019, http://www.ushistory.org/declaration/document.

104 Israel Zangwill, The Melting Pot, (New York: The Macmillan Company, 1919).

105 "The Star-Spangled Banner: The Lyrics," n.d., The Star-Spangled Banner: The Flag that Inspired the National Anthem, Accessed January 12, 2019. https://amhistory. si.edu/starspangledbanner/the-lyrics.aspX.

BIBLIOGRAPHY

"6 Lessons from the 'Founder' of McDonald's." 2017. YourStory.com. Yourstory. February 21, 2017. https://yourstory.com/mystory/3c67120cab-6-lessons-from-the-founder-of-mcdonald-s.

"9/11 Interactive Timelines." n.d. 9/11 Memorial Timeline. Accessed January 12, 2019. https://timeline.911memorial.org/#Timeline/2.

"11 Surprising Facts About *Fatal Attraction*." 2017. Mental Floss. Mental Floss. September 18, 2017. http://mentalfloss.com/article/73920/11-surprising-facts-about-fatal-attraction.

"A First." 2013. The Economist. The Economist Newspaper. March 18, 2013. https://www.economist.com/blogs/banyan/2013/03/democracy-pakistan.

"A Quote by John Emerich Edward Dalberg-Acton." n.d. Goodreads. Goodreads. Accessed January 12, 2019. https://www.goodreads.com/quotes/749222-power-corrupts-and-absolute-power-corrupts-absolutely.

Adams, John. n.d. "Letter from John Adams to Abigail Adams, 26 April 1777 [electronic edition]. Adams Family Papers: An Electronic Archive." Massachusetts Historical Society: 54th Regiment. Accessed January 12, 2019. http://www.masshist.org/digitaladams/.

"Al-Qur'an Al-Kareem." n.d. Al-Qur'an Al-Kareem. Accessed January 12, 2019. https://quran.com/3/19-20.

Baloch, Saher. 2013. "Feudal Lords Are Blocking Land Reforms." Dawn.com. November 7, 2013. https://www.dawn.com/news/1054603.

Bhunjun, Avinash. 2018. "What Does Muharram Mean and How Does the Islamic Calendar Work?" Metro. Metro.co.uk. February 1, 2018. https://metro.

co.uk/2017/09/21/what-does-muharram-mean-and-how-does-the-islamic-calendar-work-6944367/.

Butts, Dianne E. 1970. "Jesus Predicted His Own Death Three Times." Bible Prophecies Fulfilled. https://biblepropheciesfulfilled.blogspot.com/2014/03/jesus-predicted-his-own-death-three.html.

Carson, Ben, M.D. *America the Beautiful*. Grand Rapids, MI: Zondervan, 2012.

Chapman, Gary. *The Five Love Languages*. Chicago, IL: Northfield Publishing, 1992.

"Civil Rights Act of 1964 (U.S. National Park Service)." n.d. National Parks Service. U.S. Department of the Interior. Accessed January 11, 2019. https://www.nps.gov/articles/civil-rights-act.htm.

Colla, Johnny, and Huey Lewis. 1983. "The Heart of Rock and Roll." Vinyl. WB Music Corp., Huey Lewis Music, and Cause & Effect Music.

Coy, Charles. n.d. "Reward Failures to Crush Employees' Fear of Innovation." ReWork: Today's Technology Impacts Tomorrow's Talent. Accessed January 12, 2019. https://www.cornerstoneondemand.com/rework/reward-failures-crush-employees-fear-innovation.

Crossette, Barbara. 1990. "Bhutto Is Dismissed in Pakistan After 20 Months." The New York Times. The New York Times. August 7, 1990. http://www.nytimes.com/1990/08/07/world/bhutto-is-dismissed-in-pakistan-after-20-months.html?pagewanted=all.

Chowdhury, Sanchita. 2018. "The Story of Eid-Al-Adha or Bakrid." https://www.boldsky.com. Boldsky. August 20, 2018. https://www.boldsky.com/yoga-spirituality/faith-mysticism/2013/the-story-of-bakrid-035802.html.

Dudar, Hasan. 2018. "Americans Divided on Whether Immigrant Caravan Is Threat to USA." USA Today. Gannett Satellite Information Network. November 19, 2018. https://www.usatoday.com/story/news/2018/11/19/migrant-caravan-donald-trump-border-security-immigration-poll-threat-central-america-honduras/2055361002/.

Editors, *Encyclopaedia Brittannica*. 2015. "Arab Spring." *Encyclopædia Britannica*. Encyclopædia Britannica, Inc. January 14, 2015. https://www.britannica.com/event/Arab-Spring.

Editors, Dawn.com. 2018. "'Do Not Clash with the State': PM Khan Issues Stern Warning to Agitators after Aasia Bibi Verdict." Dawn.com. November 6, 2018. https://www.dawn.com/news/1442630.

Editors, History.com. 2009. "Statue of Liberty." History.com. A&E Television
 Networks. December 2, 2009. https://www.history.com/topics/landmarks/
 statue-of-liberty.

Federer, William J. *America's God and Country: Encyclopedia of Quotations.* (St. Louis:
 Amerisearch, 2000.

Franklin, Jentezen. *The Fearless Life.* Lake Mary, FL: Charisma House, 2014.

Hall, Mark David. n.d. "Did America Have a Christian Founding?" The Heritage
 Foundation. Accessed January 12, 2019. https://www.heritage.org/political-
 process/report/did-america-have-christian-founding.

Hedayat, K M, P Shooshtarizadeh, and M Raza. 2006. "Therapeutic Abortion in Islam:
 Contemporary Views of Muslim Shiite Scholars and Effect of Recent Iranian
 Legislation." *Journal of Medical Ethics.* US National Library of Medicine,
 National Institutes of Health. December 2006. https://www.ncbi.nlm.nih.gov/
 pmc/articles/PMC2563289/.

Henderson, Barney. 2017. "Indian Independence Day: Everything You Need to Know
 about Partition between India and Pakistan 70 Years On." The Telegraph.
 Telegraph Media Group. August 15, 2017. https://www.telegraph.co.uk/
 news/2017/08/15/indian-independence-day-everything-need-know-partition-
 india/.

"Invisible Hand - What Is Invisible Hand? Invisible Hand Meaning, Invisible Hand
 Definition." n.d. The Economic Times. Economic Times. Accessed January 12,
 2019. https://economictimes.indiatimes.com/definition/invisible-hand.

"Islam and Homosexuality: What Does the Koran Say?" Haaretz.com. Haaretz Com.
 May 18, 2018. https://www.haaretz.com/middle-east-news/islam-and-
 homosexuality-what-does-the-koran-say-1.5395747.

"'Islam is Peace' Says President." National Archives and Records Administration.
 National Archives and Records Administration. Accessed January
 12, 2019. https://georgewbush-whitehouse.archives.gov/news/
 releases/2001/09/20010917-11.html.

Jackson, Jason. n.d. "Ishmael or Isaac? The Koran or the Bible?" Christian Courier.
 Accessed January 12, 2019. https://www.christiancourier.com/articles/1161-
 ishmael-or-isaac-the-koran-or-the-bible.

Jackson, Wayne. n.d. "10 Great Lessons from the Book of Jonah." Christian Courier. Accessed January 12, 2019. https://www.christiancourier.com/articles/66-10-great-lessons-from-the-book-of-jonah.

Jacobs, Debra, Garrett Sheridan, and González Juan Pablo. 2011. *Shockproof: How to Hardwire Your Business for Lasting Success.* Hoboken, NJ: Wiley.

Jamal, Umair. 2017. "Zia-Ul-Haq and the 'Islamization' of Pakistan's Public Universities." The Diplomat. The Diplomat. March 28, 2017. https://thediplomat.com/2017/03/zia-ul-haq-and-the-islamization-of-pakistans-public-universities/.

"Japanese-American Internment and Redress: Petition and Coalition Building." n.d. Historical Society of Pennsylvania. Accessed January 12, 2019. https://hsp.org/education/unit-plans/japanese-american-internment/japanese-american-internment-and-redress-petition-and-coalition-building.

Karber, Phil. *Fear and Faith in Paradise.* Lanham, MD: Roman & Littlefield Publishers, Inc., 2012.

Khan, Falak Sher. n.d. "Impact of Afghan War on Pakistan." LinkedIn. Accessed January 12, 2019. https://www.linkedin.com/pulse/impact-afghan-war-pakistan-falak-sher-khan.

Kahn, Nichola. *Mohajir Militancy in Pakistan.* New York: Routledge, 2010.

Lazarus, Emma. n.d. "The New Colossus by Emma Lazarus." Poetry Foundation. Poetry Foundation. Accessed January 11, 2019. https://www.poetryfoundation.org/poems/46550/the-new-colossus.

Lewin, Tamar. 2001. "Sikh Owner Of Gas Station Is Fatally Shot In Rampage." *The New York Times.* The New York Times. September 17, 2001. https://www.nytimes.com/2001/09/17/us/sikh-owner-of-gas-station-is-fatally-shot-in-rampage.html.

Lightfoot, Neil R. *How We Got the Bible.* Grand Rapids, MI: Baker Books, 1963.

Mallouhi, Christine A. *Miniskirts, Mothers, & Muslims.* Grand Rapids, MI: Monarch Books, 2004.

McCain, John, and Mark Slater. 1999. *Faith of My Fathers.* New York, NY: Random House.

"'Military Coups in Pakistan' on Revolvy.com." n.d. Trivia Quizzes. Accessed January 12, 2019. https://www.revolvy.com/page/Military-coups-in-Pakistan.

"Muhammad: Legacy of a Prophet." PBS. Public Broadcasting Service. Accessed January 12, 2019. https://www.pbs.org/muhammad/ma_quran.shtml.

Nasr, Seyyed Hossein, and Asma Afsaruddin. 2019. "'Ali." *Encyclopædia Britannica*. Encyclopædia Britannica, Inc. January 1, 2019. https://www.britannica.com/biography/Ali-Muslim-caliph.

"Nationalization under Bhutto." 2012. History Pak. March 21, 2012. http://historypak.com/nationalization-under-bhutto.

"Naturalization Oath of Allegiance to the United States of America." n.d. 23.11 Cuban Adjustment Act Cases. | USCIS. Accessed January 12, 2019. https://www.uscis.gov/us-citizenship/naturalization-test/naturalization-oath-allegiance-united-states-america.

Niesewand, Peter. 2016. "Pakistan's Zulfikar Ali Bhutto Executed: Archive, 5 April 1979." The Guardian. Guardian News and Media. April 5, 2016. https://www.theguardian.com/world/2016/apr/05/pakistan-zulfikar-ali-bhutto-executed-1979.

"Omnist." n.d. Merriam-Webster. Merriam-Webster. Accessed January 12, 2019. https://www.merriam-webster.com/dictionary/omnist.

Paracha, Nadeem F. 2014. "Uprisings and Downfalls: Attempts at Ousting Pakistani Governments." Dawn.com. October 30, 2014. https://www.dawn.com/news/1141343.

Paracha, Nadeem F. 2016. "Karachi: What's in a Picture?" Dawn.com. July 29, 2016. https://www.dawn.com/news/1273993.

"Preamble to the U.S. Declaration of Independence, 1776." n.d. Preamble to U.S. Declaration of Independence. Accessed January 12, 2019. https://www.elcivics.com/us_declaration_preamble.html.

Press Trust of India. 2018. "Imran Khan's Swearing-In In Jeopardy As Poll Panel Withholds Notification." NDTV.com. NDTV. August 7, 2018. https://www.ndtv.com/world-news/pakistan-elections-imran-khans-swearing-in-in-jeopardy-as-pakistan-election-commission-withholds-not-1896874.

Quora. 2014. "What does Islam say about adoption?" https://www.quora.com/What-does-Islam-say-about-adoption.

Quora. 2016. "Why Are Dogs Considered Unclean and Cats Clean in Islam?" https://www.quora.com/Why-are-dogs-considered-unclean-and-cats-clean-in-Islam.

Quora. 2018. "Where Did Islam Come From?" https://www.quora.com/When-did-Islam-start.

"Religions - Islam: Abortion." 2009. BBC. BBC. September 7, 2009. http://www.bbc. co.uk/religion/religions/islam/islamethics/abortion_1.shtml.

"Religions - Islam: Five Pillars of Islam." 2009. BBC. BBC. September 8, 2009. http:// www.bbc.co.uk/religion/religions/islam/practices/fivepillars.shtml.

Saba, Sadeq. 2008. "Visiting Iran's Ayatollahs at Qom." BBC News. BBC. June 17, 2008. http://news.bbc.co.uk/2/hi/middle_east/7458709.stm.

Sciolino, Elaine. Special to *The New York Times*. 1988. "ZIA OF PAKISTAN KILLED AS BLAST DOWNS PLANE; U.S. ENVOY, 28 OTHERS DIE." *The New York Times*. *The New York Times*. August 18, 1988. https://www.nytimes. com/1988/08/18/world/zia-of-pakistan-killed-as-blast-downs-plane-us-envoy-28-others-die.html.

Silas. n.d. Wine in Islam. Accessed January 12, 2019. http://www.answering-islam.org/ Silas/no_father.htm.

Singh, Sushant. 2016. "India-Pakistan 1971 War: 13 Days That Shook the Subcontinent." The Indian Express. The Indian Express. December 16, 2016. https://indianexpress.com/article/explained/india-pakistan-1971-war-bangladesh-indira-gandhi-4429236.

"Shah Jahan Biography - Life History, Reign, Administration, Architecture, Facts." n.d. Biography - Life History, Facts, Achievements & Death. Accessed January 11, 2019. https://www.culturalindia.net/indian-history/shah-jahan.html.

"Social Customs: 'Nearly Half of Pakistani Women Are Married before the Age of 18'." 2013. The Express Tribune. The Express Tribune. August 31, 2013. https:// tribune.com.pk/story/597697/social-customs-nearly-half-of-pakistani-women-are-married-before-the-age-of-18/.

"Special Specifications of Imam Al-Mahdi (as)456." 2013. Al-Islam.org. November 12, 2013. https://www.al-islam.org/shiite-encyclopedia-ahlul-bayt-dilp-team/ special-specifications-imam-al-mahdi.

Spencer, Robert. 2017. "Pakistan: Ad for Sewer Workers 'Only for Non-Muslims.'" Jihad Watch. July 15, 2017. https://www.jihadwatch.org/2017/07/pakistan-ad-for-sewer-workers-only-for-non-muslims.

Stack, Liam. 2018. "Korean War, a Forgotten Conflict That Shaped the Modern World." The New York Times. The New York Times. January 1, 2018. https://www. nytimes.com/2018/01/01/world/asia/korean-war-history.html.

Staff, Investopedia. 2018. "Top 6 Reasons New Businesses Fail." Investopedia. Investopedia. July 9, 2018. https://www.investopedia.com/slide-show/top-6-reasons-new-businesses-fail.

Stolz, Paul G., Ph.D. *Adversity Quotient*. New York: John Wiley & Sons, Inc., 1997.

"Supreme Court Legalises 'Free-Will' Marriages." 2016. IRIN. January 7, 2016. http://www.irinnews.org/news/2003/12/30/supreme-court-legalises-free-will-marriages.

"The Declaration of Independence: Full Text." n.d. Ushistory.org. Independence Hall Association. Accessed January 12, 2019. http://www.ushistory.org/declaration/document.

"The Star-Spangled Banner: The Lyrics." n.d. The Star-Spangled Banner: The Flag that Inspired the National Anthem. Accessed January 12, 2019. https://amhistory.si.edu/starspangledbanner/the-lyrics.aspx.

Theodorou, Angelina E. 2016. "Which Countries Still Outlaw Apostasy and Blasphemy?" Pew Research Center. Pew Research Center. July 29, 2016. http://www.pewresearch.org/fact-tank/2016/07/29/which-countries-still-outlaw-apostasy-and-blasphemy.

Washington, George. n.d. "Quotes of George Washington." Accessed January 12, 2019. http://www.sonofthesouth.net/revolutionary-war/general/george-washington-quotes.htm.

"What Does It Mean to Be Unequally Yoked?" GotQuestions.org. January 9, 2019. https://www.gotquestions.org/unequally-yoked.html.

White, John. 2016. "The Hand Of God And George Washington." George Washington Inn. April 15, 2016. https://georgewashingtoninn.com/the-hand-of-god-and-george-washington.

Zafar, Ziad. 2018. "Who Killed Benazir Bhutto?" Dawn.com. December 28, 2018. https://www.dawn.com/news/1378568.

Zangwill, Israel. *The Melting Pot*. New York: The Macmillan Company, 1919.

Printed in the USA
CPSIA information can be obtained
at www.ICGtesting.com
JSHW022327140824
68134JS00019B/1331